Santa Clara County Free Library

REFERENCE

 5816

Santa Clara County Free Library

This book may be kept 14 days.

A fine of 5 cents per day will be charged on books kept overtime.

No books will be issued to persons in arrears for fines.

Books must not be loaned by the borrower.

Careful usage of books is expected, and any soiling, injury, or loss is to be paid for by the borrower.

The American Exploration and Travel Series
[For a complete list, see page 170]

ADVENTURES OF ZENAS LEONARD

Adventures of

ZENAS LEONARD

FUR TRADER

Edited by

John C. Ewers

NORMAN : UNIVERSITY OF OKLAHOMA PRESS

Books by John C. Ewers

Plains Indian Painting (Stanford, 1939)
Gustavus Sohon's Portraits of Flathead and Pend d'Oreille Indians (Washington, 1948)
The Horse in Blackfoot Indian Culture (Washington, 1955)
The Blackfeet: Raiders on the Northwestern Plains (Norman, 1958)
Adventures of Zenas Leonard, Fur Trader (editor), (Norman, 1959)

LIBRARY OF CONGRESS CATALOG CARD NUMBER: 59-7961

New edition copyright 1959 by the University of Oklahoma Press, Publishing Division of the University. Composed and printed at Norman, Oklahoma, U. S. A., by the University of Oklahoma Press. First edition.

EDITOR'S INTRODUCTION

FOR MORE THAN 230 YEARS after the founding of Quebec and Jamestown, the quest for furs provided the greatest stimulus to the white man's exploration and initial exploitation of the natural resources of the interior of North America. Far in advance of white settlements, rugged fur traders trekked over the mountains, through the Great Lakes, up and down the midwestern rivers, across the plains and the Rockies and the deserts, ever searching for beaver, the fine pelts of which were made into hats worn by fashionable ladies and gentlemen in far-off Europe and in the cities and towns of the settled East. The fur trade was the *raison d'être* of the Indian trade. It was the first and foremost business of the American wilderness.

When Upper Louisiana was formally transferred to the United States at St. Louis on March 10, 1804, the fur trade was the major business of that bustling little river town of about one thousand souls. There trading parties were equipped and dispatched to the Osage country and to distant tribes on the Missouri. Under Spanish rule, St. Louis traders had extended their operations as far up the Missouri as the Arikara villages above the mouth of Grand River in present South Dakota. Spanish authorities knew that British traders were siphoning off the peltries from the northern portion of Louisiana through their trade at the Mandan villages farther up the Missouri. They resented this British intrusion. But their feeble and fitful efforts to wrest control of the Mandan trade from their more aggressive northern rivals were of no avail. Meanwhile the beaver resources of the Arikara country were being depleted. By 1804 the returns from this area scarcely repaid the traders for the efforts they expended.

British traders had been far more aggressive in expanding their western operations than had the Spanish and French of

vii

Louisiana. Under the stimulus of keen competition between the Hudson's Bay Company and rival traders from Montreal, they had pushed up the Saskatchewan River and established posts among the powerful Blackfoot tribes in the very shadow of the Rocky Mountains. They had moved southward overland from their posts on the Assiniboine River to trade with the Mandans. Nevertheless, their receipts in fine furs from the Blackfoot and Mandan trade were small. Most of the haughty Blackfeet were little interested in trapping beaver. The returns from the Mandans were piddling. In fact, Charles Mackenzie boasted in 1806 that he was the first north trader to cross the Missouri with as many as four packs of beaver.

At the time of the transfer of Louisiana, the rich beaver country around the headwaters of the three great rivers which had their sources in the Rocky Mountains far to the south of the British posts on the Saskatchewan—the Missouri, the Columbia, and the Colorado—was still unexplored Indian territory. But when members of the Lewis and Clark expedition crossed and recrossed the Rockies on their explorations to the Pacific, they did not fail to recognize the potential importance of that region to the fur trade.

It was no accident that the first American known to have trapped the region of the Missouri headwaters was a veteran of the Lewis and Clark expedition. On their way down the Missouri homeward bound in early August, 1806, the members of William Clark's party met two young men, Forest Hancock and Joseph Dickson, who had come from Illinois on a hunting excursion. The Illinois men turned back and accompanied Clark's party to the Mandan villages. There they persuaded John Colter, one of the ablest hunters of the Lewis and Clark group, to go upriver with them and to spend the winter in trapping and trading with the Indians on the Yellowstone. Colter requested and received his commander's permission to accept the Illinois men's invitation.

John Colter's adventures as the first of the famous mountain men have become an American legend. Not only was he a member of that first American trapping party on the Yellowstone in 1806–1807, but in the next year he guided the first large fur trading expedition (led by Manuel Lisa of St. Louis) to the Yellowstone, where they built the first trading post on that river at the mouth of the Bighorn. Then, in the following winter, Colter alone crossed the Rockies and was the first white man to see the wonderlands of Jackson Hole and the present Yellowstone Park region. Colter also had the unhappy distinction of being the first American trapper to escape almost certain death at the hands of the dread Blackfeet. In the spring of 1808, he and John Potts, another veteran of the Lewis and Clark expedition, were trapping near the Three Forks of the Missouri when they were surprised by a large Blackfoot party. Potts was killed. Colter was captured, stripped of his clothes, and given a chance to run for his life. Miraculously Colter outdistanced his pursuers, jumped into the river, and hid himself so effectively in the under-brush that his enemies could not find him. Then naked, unarmed, and half-starved, he found his way back to Lisa's post at the mouth of the Bighorn.

The inveterate hostility of the Blackfeet toward American trappers continued to play a role of major importance in shaping the destiny of the Rocky Mountain fur trade. The Blackfeet did not dislike Americans without reason and they had more than one good reason for hating American trappers. Their very first meeting with Americans, in the persons of Meriwether Lewis and three enlisted men on the Two Medicine River in 1806, had resulted in bloodshed. One of the Piegans had been killed and another wounded while attempting to steal the soldiers' guns and horses. To add insult to injury, the first American trappers on the Yellowstone had made friends with the Crow Indians, tra-ditional enemies of the Blackfeet. Then the Americans had pro-ceeded to trap in the vicinity of the headwaters of the Missouri, on land which the Blackfeet considered to be theirs by right of conquest. In the eyes of the Blackfeet, American trappers were killers and robbers who were in league with their enemies. Why shouldn't they have hated the very sight of them?

In the spring of 1810, Andrew Henry and Pierre Menard, partners with Manuel Lisa in a newly formed Missouri Fur Company, built a fort on a tongue of land between the Jefferson and the Madison rivers at the Three Forks of the Missouri and attempted to trap beaver in the neighboring streams. But repeated Blackfoot attacks, in which several of the trappers were killed, convinced them of the impossibility of success in this venture. Menard, with a majority of the survivors, withdrew to Lisa's fort at the mouth of the Bighorn. Henry led a small party across the Rockies, built a post on the North Fork of Snake River, and spent the winter trapping and trading with friendly Shoshoni Indians. But the returns failed to satisfy him.

After three years of futile efforts to trap the Blackfeet-infested Three Forks area, the Missouri Fur Company decided to abandon this field. When a reorganized Missouri Fur Company tried again to trap this region in 1821 the results were even more disastrous. An enraged Blackfoot war party fell upon the trappers after they had made a successful hunt, killed their leaders, Jones and Immell, and five other whites, and carried off their furs as booty.

Twice within a period of eleven years, the Blackfeet had driven large, organized parties of American trappers out of the headwaters region of the Missouri. Yet hard-headed St. Louis traders refused to concede defeat. They seemed to be convinced that if they could send a strong enough force into this region they could combat or conciliate the Blackfeet and reap a rich harvest in beaver pelts.

In 1822 Andrew Henry, who had been driven out of the Blackfoot country twelve years earlier, was willing to give it another try. He entered into partnership with William H. Ashley to form the Rocky Mountain Fur Company. Confidently they advertised for one hundred enterprising young men to ascend the Missouri River to its source and stay there for from one to three years. Successful in recruiting the number of men sought, Henry led them up the Missouri from St. Louis. However, Assiniboin horse thieves robbed them of their horses and prevented them from reaching their destination in 1822. Henry built a post at the mouth of the Yellowstone, and his forces wintered there. Next spring they bravely set out following the main Missouri toward the Three Forks. But near the Great Falls, the Blackfeet attacked, killed four of the trappers and forced the rest to turn back to the mouth of the Yellowstone.

Meanwhile Ashley recruited another party of one hundred men and started up the Missouri in the spring of 1823. He planned to purchase horses from the Arikara and send part of his force overland to the Yellowstone. Ashley well knew the Arikaras' reputation for treachery, but he could not anticipate that, after a friendly meeting and horse trade, these Indians would attack his party at daybreak of the very day he had planned to move on. In the ensuing battle of July 2, 1823, twelve trappers were killed outright and eleven were wounded, two of them fatally. In vain Ashley sought to rally his men and urged them to push on past the Arikara villages. Most of them refused to risk another battle with the Indians. So Ashley had little choice but to drop down river to the mouth of the Teton and await reinforcements.

In response to Ashley's urgent plea for help in punishing the hostile Arikara, Colonel Henry Leavenworth, in command of 220 infantrymen with two six-pound cannon, promptly moved up the Missouri from Fort Atkinson in what was to be the Army's first campaign against the Indians west of the Mississippi River. Augmented by nearly two hundred trappers and some seven hundred Sioux Indians eager to plunder the homes of their Arikara enemies, the attacking force reached the palisaded villages of the Arikara on August 9. While the trappers and the Sioux waited for his command to attack the villages and wipe out their Arikara enemies, the Colonel hesitated and, aside from firing some cannon balls into the village, refused to take any effective action. When the Arikara sued for peace, Leavenworth offered it to them on the condition that they restore the property they had stolen from Ashley and promise peace with the whites in the future. While Leavenworth delayed, awaiting their compliance with his terms, the clever Arikara quietly abandoned their villages under cover of night.

By the fall of 1823, the Americans' prestige among the Upper Missouri tribes was at its lowest ebb. The trappers had failed repeatedly in their attempts to gain a foothold in the Blackfoot country. Ashley's large party had been defeated and turned back by the Arikara. Leavenworth's comic opera campaign to humble the Arikara had an opposite effect. The Arikara were more arrogant than ever. What is more, the powerful Sioux, who had stood by as potential allies, had only scorn and contempt for the white man's military prowess.

The traditional trapper's route up the Missouri was effectively blocked by hostile Indians. In desperation, Ashley decided to abandon the Missouri and send his trappers overland into the country of the friendly Crows and Shoshonis, long-time enemies of the troublous Blackfeet. In so doing, the men of the Rocky Mountain Fur Company detoured into a bonanza. On the headwaters of the Yellowstone, the Colorado, and the Columbia, they found beaver as plentiful as in the Blackfoot country. Under the able field leadership of such men as Jedediah Smith, David E. Jackson, William L. Sublette, and Thomas Fitzpatrick, men of the Rocky Mountain Fur Company explored the mountain wilderness south of the forbidden Blackfoot country. When the scattered trapping parties met in the mountains early in the summer of 1824, they brought with them goodly numbers of beaver pelts, which Andrew Henry subsequently took back to St. Louis.

Encouraged by the success of his Rocky Mountain venture, after two years of costly failure on the Upper Missouri, Ashley wisely adopted new methods in the operation of his mountain trade. He would rely primarily upon numerous small parties of white trappers to collect the beaver. They would go their separate ways each fall, to set their traps in the many small streams flowing from the Rockies in which beaver abounded. Instead of building and operating trading posts in the field, as the Indian traders on the Missouri had done, he would determine and appoint each summer a meeting place in one of the mountain valleys where his trappers and friendly Indians would bring their fall, winter, and spring collections the following summer. He would see to it that supplies needed to carry his men through the subsequent winter reached the predetermined rendezvous on schedule, and he would see that the year's collection of furs was transported to St. Louis. What is more, he would send trade goods for the Indians and liquor enough to permit the lonely hunters to have a high time when they gathered together at the rendezvous.

Historians have generally credited Ashley with the invention of the trappers' rendezvous. However, it seems more probable that that astute businessman adopted a pre-existing Indian custom to the needs of his business. For many years the friendly tribes of the Rocky Mountains, in whose territory the Rocky Mountain Fur Company was operating, had held an annual trading fair in one of the valleys of the Rockies. As early as 1805, the French-Canadian trader, François Larocque, had heard that the Crow Indians each spring attended a meeting with the Shoshonis, Flatheads, and other small tribes from west of the Rockies, at which they exchanged products of the plains and European manufactured goods which they had obtained at the great Mandan trading center the previous summer, for fine horses, Spanish riding gear, blankets, beads, and other articles which the Shoshoni Indians had in turn obtained from the Spanish Southwest. The rendezvous of the Rocky Mountain trappers may very well have been an adaptation and a continuation of that traditional Indian trading fair which was held in the same region long before the mountain trappers invaded the area. Certainly the tribes who attended the trappers' rendezvous of the 1820's and 1830's were the same as those who had participated in the earlier Indian fairs.

Ashley himself determined the site of the first trappers' rendezvous on Henry's Fork of Green River in the summer of 1825. In addition to his own trappers, that meeting was attended by twenty-three deserters from the service of the Hudson's Bay Company in the Columbia Valley, and some eight hundred Indians. Ashley returned from the mountains with the year's collections, which were sufficiently substantial to enable him to pay off his debts incurred during his unsuccessful venture into the Missouri River trade. At the rendezvous of 1826, Ashley sold his interests in the Rocky Mountain Fur Company to three of his ablest employees, Jedediah Smith, David Jackson, and William L. Sublette for the sum of $30,000. He retired from the trade with a comfortable fortune.

From the rendezvous of 1826 on Weber River, Jedediah Smith, leading a party of fifteen men, set out on an exploring expedition southwestward, by way of Utah Lake, the Sevier Valley, and the Virgin and Colorado rivers. From Mohave Indians he purchased a fresh supply of horses and pushed on across the hot and desolate southern California desert to San Diego. There he found that Spanish authorities looked with suspicion upon this first American party to reach California overland. However, an American sea captain aided him in purchasing supplies and in securing permission to return by the route he had followed into California.

But Smith had no intention of leaving California before he had seen much more of it. After heading eastward he turned northwestward, spent the winter hunting and trapping in the high country, and by spring reached the upper waters of the San Joaquin River. Early in May he attempted to cross the Sierra Nevada Mountains, but the deep snows made the crossing impossible. Later that month he decided to leave all of his men save two in California, and slowly moved through and over the snow across the high Sierras. Continuing across the desert wastes of the Great Basin to Great Salt Lake, he turned north and arrived at the annual rendezvous on Bear Lake on the third of July, 1827, amid the rejoicing of the mountain men who had given him up as lost.

No sooner had the rendezvous been concluded than Jedediah Smith, with eighteen men, started off again, bound for California to bring back the men he had left there the previous spring. He followed the same route he had traveled the previous summer. But Smith's second overland journey to sunny California was beset with even greater perils and difficulties than had been his first one. In the desert southwest, Mohave Indians attacked his party and killed ten of his men. Upon reaching California, he was arrested by Spanish officials and imprisoned at Monterey, until another Yankee sea captain managed to obtain his release on the condition that he would leave Mexican territory within two months.

But again Smith refused to be intimidated. Proceeding northward, he wintered on the American Fork of the Sacramento River, then moved northwestward, trapping as he went. On the Umpqua River in western Oregon, while Smith was off searching for a trail, Indians attacked his camp, killed fifteen of his men, and stole all of their furs. The three survivors fled northward. Smith continued on alone to the Hudson's Bay Company post at Fort Vancouver on the Columbia. There Dr. John McLoughlin, the factor, not only received him courteously but sent men to recover most of Smith's furs stolen by the Indians, and then bought the furs from him at a fair price.

After wintering at Fort Vancouver, Smith traveled eastward up the Columbia to the Hudson's Bay Company post among the Flatheads, then southward to rejoin his partners on Henry's Fork of the Snake River. On this long journey he had been gone for very nearly two years.

Jedediah Smith's two expeditions to California in the years 1826–29 added greatly to American knowledge of the Far West beyond the Rockies and won him a deserved reputation as the greatest explorer among the hardy, restless, mountain men. Strangely enough, in spite of the loss of twenty-five men from Indian attacks and the hardships experienced by its leader, the second expedition had been a profitable fur-trade venture.

At the rendezvous of 1830 on Wind River or its tributary, the Popo Agie, the partners Smith, Jackson, and Sublette sold their interests in the Rocky Mountain Fur Company to a group of five younger men, all of whom were able, active, and experienced mountain men—Thomas Fitzpatrick, Milton G. Sublette,

Henry Fraeb, Jean Baptiste Gervais, and James Bridger. That rendezvous was noteworthy also because it was the first to be supplied by wagons. William Sublette left St. Louis on April 10 with a caravan of ten wagons and two dearborns drawn by mules. He followed the route up the Platte to the mountains which was later to become known as the Oregon Trail, and arrived at the rendezvous on July 16.

In the year 1831, Zenas Leonard entered the fur trade of the Rocky Mountains in the employ of a rival firm. But the Rocky Mountain Fur Company, which had pioneered in the development of the trade in this region, was still the dominant organization in the Rockies. However, its success was well known and had attracted many competitors. Not only were numerous small parties of free trappers roaming the mountains searching for beaver sign, but the great American Fur Company, which had previously been content to operate Indian trading posts on the Missouri, was making a serious bid for a goodly share of the profits in the mountain trade. It became an active competitor in 1829 when Henry Vandenburgh led a party of thirty hunters supplied with beaver traps from St. Louis to the Rockies.

By the summer of 1832, their rivals considerably outnumbered the men of the Rocky Mountain Fur Company. At the rendezvous in Pierre's Hole that year, there were about one hundred employees of the Rocky Mountain Fur Company. But there were also some ninety men of the American Fur Company, a large, uncounted number of free trappers, and eight or ten men in the command of Nathaniel J. Wyeth, a greenhorn from Boston. At that very time, another newcomer to the trade, Captain Benjamin L. E. Bonneville, was approaching the mountains at the head of a party of one hundred and ten men, guided by two experienced assistants, Joseph Reddeford Walker and M. S. Cerré.

It is interesting to recall that only ten years earlier, when the Upper Missouri and not the Rocky Mountains had been the goal of ambitious St. Louis traders, this rich fur land had been largely unknown to, and unexplored by, white men. Before the end of another decade its streams were nearly denuded of beaver. The last rendezvous of the mountain trappers was held on Green River in 1839. Thereafter, many of the leaders of the mountain men found employment guiding overland emigrant trains or government exploring expeditions. But in the early 1830's, when Zenas Leonard became one of them, the mountain men were still kings in the rugged domain of the Rockies.

Zenas Leonard—from Farm Boy to Mountain Man

The lure of adventure in the fur trade of the Rockies attracted hundreds of restless, vigorous young men from a wide variety of localities and from different economic and social backgrounds. Some of them came from far off Ireland, England, and Scotland, or from the continent of Europe. Some of them came south from Canada to seek greater opportunities in the expanding American trade. But the great majority of the fur trade recruits were Americans from the East and the Middle West. Some of them were men who had committed crimes or got into trouble, who moved west in a hurry to avoid punishment, and who dared not return home. But a goodly number were young men of good families from the small towns and rural communities of Kentucky, Tennessee, western Virginia, and Pennsylvania. Their experiences in rugged outdoor living in the Appalachians helped to prepare them for the many hardships they were to encounter in the higher, wilder Rocky Mountains. One of these young men was Zenas Leonard of Clearfield County, Pennsylvania.

Zenas Leonard was of hardy, pioneer stock. His paternal grandfather, Patrick Leonard, had migrated from Ireland to Pennsylvania before the Revolutionary War. For a time he traded with the Indians at the site of present Harrisburg and as far up the Susquehanna as Sunbury. Then he settled down to farming. Zenas Leonard's father, Abraham, was born near Harrisburg on July 11, 1777. He became a frontier farmer. In 1803, the year before Clearfield County, Pennsylvania, was created, he traveled northwestward to that area. He liked it so well that he returned the next spring with his wife, Elizabeth Armstrong Leonard, and their three children. Near the mouth of Clearfield Creek he made his clearing and planted his crops.

There Zenas Leonard was born on March 19, 1809. He was one of nine children raised on the Leonard farm. In family tradition, Zenas is remembered as a wild, carefree, dare-devil youth. He received a common grade-school education, but he undoubtedly found greater enjoyment hunting deer, bear, and other game in the woods than he did studying in the schoolroom. There can be no doubt that he learned to handle a rifle well. But the humdrum life of a farmer in the rocky Alleghenies held no attraction for him. It is said that on the morning of his twenty-first birthday Zenas informed his father, "I can make my living without picking stones." His father replied that he was at liberty to do so.

So Zenas packed his few belongings and walked to Pittsburgh, where one of his mother's brothers was a merchant. For several months Zenas clerked in his uncle's establishment. Then he again became restless. He had heard of the opportunities for adventure in the western fur trade. So Zenas again packed and moved —on down the Ohio to St. Louis, the great emporium of the fur trade and the embarkation point for overland trapping and trading expeditions bound for the fabulous Rocky Mountains. There he was engaged as a clerk in the firm of Gantt and Blackwell, which had ambitions to compete with the Rocky Mountain Fur Company and the American Fur Company for the fur trade of the Rockies.

Zenas Leonard's own account of his adventures in the fur trade of the Rocky Mountains and beyond begins with his departure from St. Louis on April 24, 1831, with the Gantt and Blackwell party. His narrative tells of the frightful hardships in the first winter's trapping venture on Laramie River, after which the Gantt and Blackwell partnership was dissolved; of his experiences as a free trapper in the Rockies in 1832 and 1833; of his meeting with Captain Bonneville's party at the rendezvous on Green River in July of 1833; of the expedition overland to California in 1833 commanded by Bonneville's lieutenant, Joseph Reddeford Walker, which Leonard accompanied as clerk, and of the expedition's return to Bonneville's rendezvous on Bear River a year later; of his hunting and trapping experiences as a Bonneville employee in the Crow country of the Yellowstone and Wind River valleys in the fall and winter of 1834–35. Leonard's narrative of his adventures concludes with his return to Independence, Missouri, with Captain Bonneville on August 29, in the year 1835.

Leonard returned from the mountains with but $1,100 to show for more than four years of hard work and privations during which he had repeatedly risked his life in combat with hostile Indians and against the forces of nature. When he reached Clearfield in the fall of 1835, his family was overjoyed to see him. They had received no word from him since he left St. Louis on his outward journey, and they feared he had been killed. Nevertheless, they took little stock in his "tall tales" of his western adventures.

Zenas Leonard remained home for a period of about six months. Then he turned westward again. According to family tradition, he took with him several ox teams and wagons loaded with supplies. On the site of old Fort Osage (which Leonard had passed on his way to the Rockies in 1831), at present Sibley, Missouri, Leonard established a store. He catered to the settlers in the local community and sold outfits to traders moving west. He also operated a boat between Cogswell landing and St. Louis, by which he shipped furs, which he obtained through trading with the Indians, to the market in St. Louis and brought back goods and merchandise.

Leonard married Isabel Harrelson, a Kentucky girl some sixteen years his junior, who had migrated to Missouri with her parents. They became the parents of three children, Zenas, Martha, and Elizabeth. Zenas Leonard died on July 14, 1857, at the age of 48. He was buried in the old Sibley Cemetery. The Jackson County Historical Society in 1959 was planning to erect a fitting marker at the grave of Zenas Leonard—mountain man, explorer, and chronicler of some of the most stirring episodes in the history of the Old West.

Zenas Leonard's Narrative

Very few among the hundreds of mountain trappers who ranged the Rocky Mountains in the years 1831 to 1835 left any permanent record of their rich experiences in the fur trade. The very great majority of these men were much handier with rifles and traps than with pens or pencils. The fascinating stories they must have told of their travels and explorations, of their bitter encounters with hostile Indians, and of the dangers they encountered almost daily in their hazardous occupation, as well as the observations they must have made upon the country, its wild life, and its people, died with them.

Zenas Leonard, however, was an outstanding exception in that he not only wrote down his experiences and observations during the more than four years that he was in the Rockies and beyond, but he also published them within five years of his return from the mountains.

We know nothing of the circumstances under which Leonard came to write his *Narrative* other than the tantalizingly brief statement of his editor and publisher, D. W. Moore, in his preface to the original edition of the work. Moore indicates that Zenas Leonard was induced to write his *Narrative* in response to the widespread interest in his western experiences among his friends and acquaintances in the neighborhood of Clearfield, Pennsylvania, and that the first installments of his account first were printed in the newspapers of Clearfield County. This portion of Leonard's *Narrative* covered only a small part of the whole. It described his travels from St. Louis to the Laramie River, and his first winter in the West, hunting and trapping in the valley of the Laramie.

Moore's statement that he did not procure the Leonard manuscript until the winter of 1838–39 might suggest that Leonard did not complete the writing of the latter portion of it much before that time. If that was the case, Leonard probably had an opportunity to read Washington Irving's *The Rocky Mountains: or Scenes, Incidents, and Adventures in the Far West; from the Journal of Captain Benjamin L. E. Bonneville, U.S.A., in the Rocky Mountains and the Far West*, which was published in 1837. Leonard made no reference to that work in his *Narrative*. Nevertheless, Bonneville's disparaging remarks about the Walker expedition to California and his defamation of the character of its leader, as recorded by Irving, may have encouraged Leonard to place on record his quite different interpretation of that expedition and of the actions and abilities of Walker.

The entire Leonard *Narrative* was first published in the columns of Moore's newspaper, *The Clearfield Republican*, in serial form, then, in response to popular demand, Moore reprinted the complete account in more convenient form. This little volume of eighty-seven pages, cheaply printed in two columns of not undistinguished type, bears the quaint title, *Narrative of the Adventures of Zenas Leonard, a native of Clearfield County, Pa. who spent five years in trapping for furs, trading with the Indians, &c., &c., of the Rocky Mountains: written by himself*, and the imprint *Printed and published by D. W. Moore, Clearfield, Pa. 1839*

As a relation of the experiences of an active participant in the fur trade of the Rocky Mountains and beyond, Leonard's *Narrative* appears to be the revelation of an honest, average man who resisted any temptation to portray himself as the hero of every exciting adventure. The Zenas Leonard of the *Narrative* was no superman. He was a plausible human being. Frankly, he admitted his longing for the comforts of home when he suffered pangs of hunger in the dead of winter on the Laramie River. When he fought in the battle of Pierre's Hole, he was fearful lest he might perform some act of cowardice. And later, when alone and armed only with a knife, he encountered a lone Indian with a bow and arrow, he wisely ran for his life. If Leonard was a man of little humor, he certainly was not a griper either. He was loyal both to his comrades and to his leaders, and fair in his judgments of the actions of other men.

As a description of the country, its natural resources, and the peoples who inhabited it, Leonard's *Narrative* is the writing of a good observer. If he did not describe his whereabouts at all times in terms that are precise and understandable to us today, we must remember that he and his companions ranged widely over a broad area which was strange to them and in which the landmarks were nameless save to the local Indians, whose languages they did not comprehend. Sometimes he erred in referring to the names of rivers he had not seen or in describing Indian customs which he had heard about but had not seen with his own eyes. His descriptions of the material culture and overt behavior of the Indians and Spanish-Mexicans, based upon sight impressions, are clear and precise. Leonard's explanations of Crow Indian hunting and fighting methods are valuable contributions to the ethnology of that tribe. However, his accounts of their political organization and religion appear to be oversimplifications based upon incomplete knowledge of these complex aspects of Indian life.

Leonard's publisher claimed that he had kept a journal during his years in the West but that part of it was stolen from him by hostile Indians. A considerable portion of the *Narrative* must have been written from memory. This may account for many inaccuracies in the dating of events and some errors in the spelling of proper names. Nevertheless, as a history of the exploration and exploitation of the West during the period of intensified activity in the mountain fur trade of the early 1830's, Leonard's *Narrative* is of permanent value. It has been quoted frequently by historians of the western fur trade.

Historians regard Leonard's first-hand observations during the overland expedition to California of 1833–34 under the command of Joseph Reddeford Walker as the most complete and accurate account of that first American exploration westward to the Pacific by way of the Sierra Nevada Mountains. Half of Leonard's *Narrative* comprises a report of that significant expedition.

Leonard's conception of instructions given the leader of that expedition and of Walker's abilities as a leader are at variance with the estimates of Captain Bonneville, Walker's superior, who dispatched him on that journey of exploration. Leonard believed Walker was told to explore westward to the Pacific in search of beaver. He considered Walker an exceedingly able commander who exercised prudence and good judgment even under the most trying conditions. Bonneville, on the other hand, berated Walker for exceeding his authority in exploring westward beyond the Great Salt Lake, for attacking and murdering inoffensive Digger Indians in the Great Basin, and for prodigally wasting the company's resources in unprofitable and unnecessary amusements in distant California.

In attempting to evaluate Bonneville's vilifications of Walker, we should consider the subsequent relations between these men. Had Bonneville been as incensed with Walker's actions at the time the latter returned from California as he later led Washington Irving to believe he had been, surely he would have dismissed his lieutenant on the spot. Instead, as Leonard's *Narrative* clearly indicates, Bonneville placed Walker in charge of his important fur-trade operations in the Crow country during the following winter. Cleverly, Bonneville disguised this fact in the information he gave to Irving by referring to his deputy among the Crows in the winter of 1833–34 by the Spanish name (or nickname) of "Montero" (The Huntsman). There can be little doubt that Walker and Montero were one and the same man.

When Bonneville returned east and had to explain the financial failure of his three years' venture in the western fur trade to his backers in New York, he must have found it quite convenient to blame Walker's "disgraceful expedition" to California for his lack of success.

Because Zenas Leonard's *Narrative* is an interesting adventure story as well as a significant description and history of the mountain fur trade and exploration in the Old West, copies of the rare first edition of this work have been avidly sought by book collectors. They have been known to bring as much as $3,500 in the market.

The *Narrative* has twice been reprinted in limited editions. In 1904 it appeared under the title *Adventures of Zenas Leonard, Fur Trader and Trapper, 1831–1836,* edited by W. F. Wagner. It was reprinted under the title *Narrative of the Adventures of Zenas Leonard,* edited by Milo Milton Quaife, in 1934. This third reprinting of a deservedly famous classic in the literature of the Old West has been made from a copy of the original edition in the Rare Book Room of the Library of Congress in Washington. Acknowledgment is due that great library for permission to photostat the entire work for use in preparing this volume.

John C. Ewers

Arlington, Virginia
April 14, 1959

EDITOR'S ACKNOWLEDGMENTS

IT IS A PLEASURE to acknowledge the kind assistance of the many others who helped to make this book possible. In my quest for additional information regarding the author, Zenas Leonard, Miss Inez Crandle, librarian, Joseph and Elizabeth Shaw Public Library, Clearfield, Pennsylvania, provided valuable leads. Three members of the Leonard family, Mrs. Genevieve Smith and James Leonard of Clearfield, and the latter's son, Alvin O. Leonard of Spartanburg, South Carolina, furnished information regarding Zenas Leonard's ancestry and his early life in Clearfield. Kenneth B. Holmes of the State Historical Society, Columbia, Missouri, and W. Howard Adams of Blue Springs, Missouri, who is President of the Jackson County Historical Society, supplied data on Leonard's later years in Missouri.

Herman R. Friis, chief, Cartographic Records Division, the National Archives, and Miss Elizabeth Wellshear, librarian, Denver Branch, U. S. Geological Survey, aided my search for appropriate illustrations.

I am also indebted to the members of the staffs of the Library of Congress and the library of the Smithsonian Institution for making printed source materials on the history of the fur trade readily accessible to me.

J. C. E.

PREFACE TO THE FIRST EDITION

THE TITLE of the following work sufficiently explains itself; however, before presenting it to the public, in its present form, the publisher deems it necessary to accompany it with a few remarks explanatory of the motives which induced the author to commit his adventures to paper:

Mr. Zenas Leonard (the author) is a native of Clearfield County, Pa., where his parents and other relatives still reside; and it may not be improper here to remark, that they are well known as among the most respectable inhabitants of the county.

After receiving the advantages of a common English education, and being possessed of strong mental faculties and a vigorous constitution, Mr. Leonard left his parental roof in the spring of 1830, and after spending the succeeding year in a mercantile house in Pittsburgh, Pa., ventured to embark in an expedition across the Rocky Mountains, in the capacity of clerk to the company. The last letter received by his parents, left him at the extreme white settlement, where they were busily occupied in making preparations for the expedition to the mountains—from whence he promised to write at short intervals; but one misfortune after another happening to the company, he was deprived of all sources of communication—so that no tidings were received of him until he unexpectedly returned to the scenes of his childhood, to the house of his father, in the fall of 1835—after an absence of five years and six months!

In the interval, and at various times, rumors and answers to letters written by his friends to different individuals on the route up the Missouri, were received, which represented the major part of the company he was with, as having perished, and that he was not among the number who survived. The grief of his parents from that time until his joyous return, can only be imagined. They had long mourned him as lost forever, and all hope of again meeting him this side the grave ceased to exist. The Scriptural phrase, that "the dead's alive, and the lost is found," in a temporal point of view, was never more beautifully illustrated; nor was ever grief and mourning changed to inexpressible joy and gladness more unexpectedly and triumphantly.

After again mingling with his former comrades and old acquaintances, so great was the curiosity manifested by them to hear him relate his adventures, that he was continually beset by crowds of anxious inquirers wherever he happened to be. But few were satisfied with a partial account, and finding that it would consume too much of the time he purposed spending among his former friends, ere he should again embark for the west, to repeat the whole story on every occasion, he finally yielded to the importunities of his friends to adopt Franklin's notion of "saying grace over the whole barrel of beef at once, in order to save time," and he prepared a narrative of his travels for publication in the newspapers of the county, that all might have an equal opportunity to read it. It was for this purpose, and under these circumstances, that he wrote it out—but from various causes it was never published entire, until we procured the manuscript last winter and gave it to the public through the columns of a public newspaper during the past season. The great interest the public took in it, was satisfactorily illustrated by the increase and demand for the paper in which it was published. A number of persons sent in their names as subscribers from all the adjoining counties, besides others more distant—many of whom we were unable to accommodate. From this evidence, as well as the repeated solicitations from every quarter, we have been induced to reprint it, and now offer it to the public in a more convenient form.

Our author kept a minute journal of every incident that occurred, but unfortunately, a part of his narrative was stolen from him by hostile Indians; still, however, he was enabled to replace the most important events, by having access to the journal kept by the commander of the expedition. His character for candour

and truth, among his acquaintances, we have never heard sus-
pected; and, indeed, among the many who heard the narrative
from his own lips, we have yet to hear the first one say they
disbelieve it. At all events, in its perusal, the reader will encounter no *improbabilities*, much less *impossibilities*:—hence it
is but reasonable to suppose that in traversing such a wilderness as lays west of the Rocky Mountains, such hardships, privations and dangers as those described by Mr. Leonard, must
necessarily be encountered.

He remained at home but a short time, when he returned to
the west, and now resides in Jackson County, Mo., where he
is surrounded with competence—being at present engaged as a
merchant and trader with the different companies employed in
the fur trade of the mountains.

THE PUBLISHER

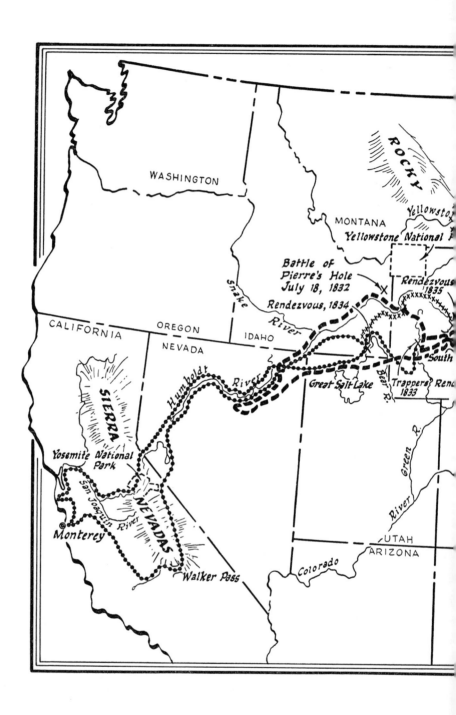

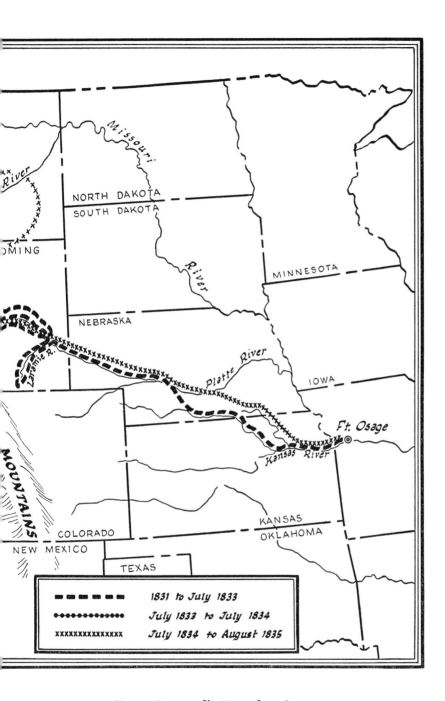

Zenas Leonard's Travels, 1831–35

CONTENTS

ILLUSTRATIONS

ADVENTURES OF ZENAS LEONARD

NARRATIVE

Of the adventures of a company of 70 men, who left St. Louis in the spring of 1831, on an expedition to the Rocky Mountains, for the purpose of trapping for furs, and trading with the Indians, by one of the company, Mr. Zenas Leonard, of Clearfield County, Pa.—comprising a minute description of the incidents of the adventure, and a valuable history of this immense territory—not from maps and charts, but from personal observation.

The company under the command of Captains Gant and Blackwell, left St. Louis on the 24th of April, 1831.[1] Each man was furnished with the necessary equipments for the expedition —such as traps, guns, &c.; also horses and goods of various descriptions, to trade with the Indians for furs and buffalo robes. We continued our journey in a western direction, in the state of Missouri, on the south side of the Missouri river, through a country thinly inhabited by the whites and friendly Indians, until we arrived at Fort Osage the extreme point of the white settlement.[2] Here we remained several days and purchased and packed up a sufficiency of provision, as we then thought, for our subsistence through the wilderness to what is called the buf-

[1] Very little is known of this firm. It built a post on the Upper Arkansas, some six miles above Fountain Creek, in 1832. Captain John Gantt was an experienced trapper and Indian trader whose operations among the Arapaho Indians in Colorado were more successful than his venture into the Wyoming country in which Zenas Leonard participated.

[2] Fort Osage was built by General William Clark in the fall of 1808 on the Missouri River twenty-four miles east of the mouth of the Kansas. It was the westernmost military post of the United States until Fort Atkinson was established at Council Bluffs in 1819–1820. It served as a government trading post for Indians until 1822. When Jackson County, Missouri, was organized in 1827, the logs of the old fort were appropriated by settlers for use in constructing homes.

3

falo country; a distance of about two hundred miles. From thence we proceeded up the Missouri until we arrived at the mouth of the Kanzas river, where we again tarried two or three days, for the purpose of trading some goods to the Kanzas Indians for corn, moccasins, &c.

This tribe of Indians live in small huts, built of poles, covered with straw and dirt, and in shape similar to a potato hole. They cultivate the soil quite extensively, and raise very good corn, pumpkins, beans and other vegetables. The principal chief is called "*White Ploom.*"[3]— The nation is supposed to contain eight hundred warriors.[4]

From thence we proceeded on our journey up the river. We found the country here beautiful indeed—abounding with the most delightful prairies, with here and there a small brook, winding its way to the river, the margins of which are adorned with the lofty pine and cedar tree. These prairies were completely covered with fine low grass, and decorated with beautiful flowers of various colors; and some of them are so extensive and clear of timber and brush that the eye might search in vain for an object to rest upon. I have seen beautiful and enchanting sceneries depicted by the artist, but never anything to equal the work of rude nature in those prairies. In the spring of the year when the grass is green and the blossoms fresh, they present an appearance, which for beauty and charms, is beyond the art of man to depict.

We continued on our journey westward, up the Republican fork of Kanzas River—passing through these prairies, till the 20th of June, when we happened on another tribe of Indians,

[3] Chief White Plume was renowned for his friendship toward the whites. In 1821 he visited Washington, where his portrait was painted by Charles Bird King. He was the first signer of the treaty between the Kansa Indians and the United States of June 3, 1825. When Alfred Jacob Miller painted his portrait in 1837, White Plume made sure that the artist showed the silver medal given him by President John Quincy Adams suspended from a chain around his neck. Marvin Ross, *The West of Alfred Jacob Miller*, Plate 17.

[4] This number appears excessive. The entire population of the Kansas was estimated at 1,200 in 1829 and 1,588 fourteen years later. F. W. Hodge (ed.), *Handbook of American Indians North of Mexico*, I, 654.

4

called the Otoes, from whom we obtained a quantity of sweet corn and some wild turnips; we also understood from this tribe that it was much farther to the buffalo country than we had before anticipated, and that game in that direction was very scarce. From thence we proceeded in a N.W. direction, up the Republican Branch—finding but very little game; and on the 21st of June we killed our last beef, which was equally divided to each mess. Here we began to feel somewhat alarmed—starvation began to stare us in the face, and some of the company became refractory and were for turning back. Stimulated, however, by the hope of reaching game in a few days, we continued in the direction of the buffalo country. Hunters were sent out daily in quest of game, but as often returned without any. We still continued to travel—subsisting chiefly on mussels and small fish which we caught in the river; finally the Captain ordered two of the best horses to be killed, to keep the company from starving, which was immediately done, and the carcasses equally distributed to each mess. We proceeded on our journey slowly—sending out hunters as usual, but without success; game appeared to become scarcer and scarcer, and in a few days our provision (if I may call it such) again exhausted. Finding it impossible, owing to the scarcity of game, to continue any further up the Republican, we concluded to leave it and steer for the headwaters of the Missouri.[5] Accordingly we changed our direction as well as our manner of traveling. Instead of traveling in a close mat as heretofore, we now scattered over a considerable range of country for the purpose of hunting, leaving ten or twelve men only to bring on the pack-mules, and at night we would collect together with our game, which generally consisted of wolves, wild cats, mussels, and some times an antelope. In this way we continued our journey slowly, some of the company being half starved to death, for eight or ten days, eating at night what little game we caught through the day; at last we collected one evening, I think about the middle of July, in a barren prairie where

[5] The author must have intended to say the Platte River rather than the Missouri.

5

we could not get wood enough to make a fire, much less anything to cook on it—not a mouthful of game was returned that evening. This was a trying time indeed—despondency and horror were depicted in the countenance of every man, and the enquiry, "what shall we do," was passing from every lip. In this condition, without fire or food, we spent the night. In the morning we held a consultation to decide whether to continue in that direction or turn. We finally agreed to proceed straight ahead and by night we arrived on the banks of the river Platte, a distance of about ten miles from where we had encamped the night before, where we pitched our tents for the night. Most of our hunters had collected without game and pronounced it very scarce, and we were about to kill another of our horses, when we saw one of our hunters approaching us with unusual rapidity, without his gun or hat and his countenance indicating great excitement. I never wish to feel more pleasure than I did as he rushed into the tent exclaiming, "I have killed two big buck elk!" Early the next morning—refreshed with what meat we had obtained and animated and encouraged with the hope of obtaining plenty more, we set out with unusual fine spirits. We continued to travel up the river Platte for several days—passing through extensive barren prairies, the soil being too poor even to produce grass; and game exceedingly scarce. Some of us again became alarmed, and one morning when the roll was called it was discovered that two of the company had stolen two of the best horses and started back to the state of Missouri. This had a bad effect—it impaired that full confidence which had heretofore existed between the members of the company, but we continued up the river and in a few days arrived at the buffalo country. After encamping, on a pleasant evening, in the latter part of July, some of the company discovered two buffalo bulls feeding in the prairie, about half a mile from camp. Four or five of us immediately mounted our horses and started to take them; but returned in a short time without success—one of the men having got his arm broken, by falling from his horse. But the next day we happened on a large drove of these animals, and killed six or seven of them. The flesh of the buffalo is the wholesomest and most palatable of meat kind. The male of these animals are much the largest—weighing from one thousand to fifteen hundred pounds, and may be seen in droves of hundreds feeding in the plains. We remained here several days feasting upon buffalo meat. From thence proceeded up the river; finding an abundance of game, such as buffalo, elk, deer and antelope—and killing more or less every day. On the first day of August we arrived at the forks of the river Platte; and by means of boats made of buffalo skins, crossed the South Fork and continued our journey up the valley. Here the soil appeared to be very poor, producing but little grass; and in some places for three or four miles we would travel over sand plains where there was scarcely a spear of grass to be seen. Immediately on the water courses the soil is better and produces good grass. As we traveled up the river, we occasionally came in contact with cliffs of rocks and hard clay, from two to three hundred feet above the level of the plain. One of these cliffs is very peculiar in its appearance, and is known among the whites as "Chimney Cliff," and among the natives as "Elk Peak." It is only about 150 yards in circumference at its basis, and about 25 at the summit; and projects into the air to the height of 300 feet. Its towering summit may be seen at the distance of fifteen or twenty miles—presenting the appearance of some huge fabric that had been constructed by the art of man.[6]

We continued to travel in a western direction—found game plenty—met with no difficulty in getting along; and on the 27th of August we arrived at the junction of the Laramies River with the river Platte—about 12 or 1,300 miles from the United States, and two or three hundred from the top of the Rocky Mountains.[7]

[6] Chimney Rock, located on the south side of the Platte River, about twenty-three miles east of present Scotts Bluff National Monument in Nebraska, was one of the most noteworthy landmarks on the Oregon Trail. It was referred to in hundreds of journals and diaries of traders, trappers, and emigrants who traveled westward up the Platte. Alfred Jacob Miller probably was the first of many artists to sketch it. See Merrill J. Mattes, "Chimney Rock on the Oregon Trail," *Nebraska History*, Vol. XXXVI, No. 1 (1955), 1–26.

[7] Laramie River was named after Jacques La Ramée, who, according to tradition, was killed by Indians in 1821 while trapping on this stream. In 1834

Here we stopped for the purpose of reconnoitering. Several scouting parties were sent out in search of beaver signs, who returned in a few days and reported that they had found beaver signs, &c. Captain Gant then gave orders to make preparations for trapping. Accordingly the company was divided into parties of fifteen to twenty men in each party, with their respective captains placed over them—and directed by Captain Gant in what direction to go. Captain Washburn ascended the Timber Fork; Captain Stephens the Laramies; Captain Gant the Sweet Water —all of which empty into the river Platte near the same place. Each of these companies were directed to ascend these rivers until they found beaver sufficiently plenty for trapping, or till the snow and cold weather compelled them to stop; at which event they were to return to the mouth of the Laramies River, to pass the winter together. While at this place, engaged in secreting our merchandise, which we did by digging a hole in the ground sufficiently large to contain them, and covering them over so that the Indians might not discover them—four men (three whites and one Indian) came to our tent. This astonished us not a little, for a white man was the last of living beings that we expected to visit us in this vast wilderness—where nothing was heard from dark to daylight but the fierce and terrifying growls of wild beasts, and the more shrill cries of the merciless savages. The principal of these men was a Mr. Fitzpatrick, who had been engaged in trapping along the Columbia River, on the west side of the Rocky Mountains, and was then on his way to St. Louis.[8] He was an old hand at the business and we ex-

William Sublette and Robert Campbell built Fort William at the mouth of this river. Under the name of Fort Laramie this and subsequent structures on the site became famous as a center for Indian trade, a way station for overland emigrants and exploring expeditions, and a military post during the Plains Indian wars. Fort Laramie National Monument was established to protect and preserve this historic site in 1938.

[8] Thomas Fitzpatrick, who at that time was one of the partners in the Rocky Mountain Fur Company, has been called the greatest of the mountain men. Born in County Cavan, Ireland, in 1799, he came to America before he was 17 and drifted west to become an Indian trader. He was a member of William Ashley's second expedition up the Missouri in 1823 which was defeated by the Arikaras. Diverted to the Rocky Mountains, he played a prominent role in the

pected to obtain some useful information from him, but we were disappointed. The selfishness of man is often disgraceful to human nature; and I never saw more striking evidence of this fact, than was presented in the conduct of this man Fitzpatrick. Notwithstanding we had treated him with great friendship and hospitality, merely because we were to engage in the same business with him, which he knew we never could exhaust or even impair —he refused to give us any information whatever, and appeared disposed to treat us as intruders. On the 3d of September, Captain Blackwell, with two others, joined Fitzpatrick, and started back to the state of Missouri, for an additional supply of merchandise, and were to return in the summer of 1832.

I was one of 21 that composed the company under the command of Captain A. K. Stephens, a man well calculated to pilot or manage in case of difficulty with the Indians. He received a portion of the profits arising from the merchandise, say two dollars per pound for coffee, and the same for tea, sugar, lead, powder, tobacco, allspice, pepper, &c., and for every yard of coarse cloth ten dollars, and for fine cloth twenty dollars; this, however, is governed entirely by their value with the Indians. For twenty or thirty loads of powder you can generally get from eight to twelve dollars worth of fur.

explorations and successful operations of the Rocky Mountain Fur Company during the next twelve years. He became a full partner in the firm in 1830. In 1835, after the dissolution of his company, Fitzpatrick entered the employ of his former rival, the American Fur Company. After the decline of the mountain fur trade, he served as guide to such famous missionary and military expeditions as those of Father Pierre Jean De Smet, Captain John C. Frémont, Colonel Stephen W. Kearny, and Lieutenant James W. Abert. He was appointed Indian Agent of the Upper Platte and Arkansas in 1846. He served as a commissioner at the important Fort Laramie Treaty of 1851, and as sole commissioner at the treaty with the Comanches, Kiowas, and other southern tribes negotiated at Fort Atkinson in 1853. He died in Washington, D. C., on February 7, 1854, while in the capital city on Indian Service business. The active and successful career of this able trapper, trader, guide, and Indian Agent is traced in LeRoy R. Hafen and W. J. Ghent, *Broken Hand: The Life of Thomas Fitzpatrick, Chief of the Mountain Men*.

However, Leonard's memory of this meeting with Fitzpatrick was faulty. At that season in 1831, Fitzpatrick was en route northward from Santa Fe to join his partners and to winter on Powder River. He had not come from the Columbia, and was not bound for St. Louis.

9

On the 4th of September, having everything in readiness, after shaking hands all round, we separated, each party to meander the rivers that had been respectively allotted to them, with with the intention, if nothing happened to them, of re-assembling in the latter part of December, to spend the winter together.

Mr. Stephens' party commenced their tour up the Laramies River and continued several days without any important occurrence. Found the prairies or plains in this direction very extensive—unobstructed with timber or brush—handsomely situated, with here and there a small creek passing through them, and in some places literally covered with game, such as buffalo, white and black tailed deer, grizzly, red, and white bear, elk, prairie dog, wild goat, big horned mountain sheep, antelope, &c.

On the 20th of September we stopped on the bank of a small creek to let our horses graze, at the junction of which we seen signs of beaver. Two hunters were sent up this stream with their traps and guns on search of beaver who, if they should be successful in finding game, were not to return till the next day—the main body of the company to move on slowly. After traveling several miles, and hearing nothing of our hunters, we deemed it advisable to encamp for the night, which we did. About midnight we were alarmed by the report of two rifles. Supposing it to be hostile Indians, we put ourselves in an attitude of defense, as soon as possible by throwing up a fort of logs and brush, and keeping up sentinels until morning. On the next morning, about sunrise the two hunters came in and informed us that it was the report of their guns that had alarmed us, as they had fired them off near the spot where they had expected to find the camp, with the hope of receiving some signal. They had meandered the creek till they came to beaver dams, where they set their traps and turned their horses out to pasture; and were busily engaged in constructing a camp to pass the night in, when they discovered, at a short distance off, a tremendous large grizzly bear rushing upon them at a furious rate. They immediately sprang to their rifles, which were standing against a tree hard-by, one of which was single and the other double triggered; unfortunately in the hurry, the one that was accustomed to the single trigger, caught up the double triggered gun, and when the bear came upon him, not having set the trigger, he could not get his gun off; and the animal approaching within a few feet of him, he was obliged to commence beating it over the head with his gun. Bruin, thinking this rather rough usage, turned his attention to the man with the single triggered gun, who, in trying to set the trigger (supposing he had the double triggered gun) had fired it off, and was also obliged to fall to beating the ferocious animal with his gun; finally, it left them without doing much injury, except tearing the sleeve off one of their coats and biting him through the hand. Four men were immediately dispatched for the traps, who returned in the evening with seven or eight beaver. The grizzly bear is the most ferocious animal that inhabits these prairies, and are very numerous. They no sooner see you than they will make at you with open mouth. If you stand still, they will come within two or three yards of you, and stand upon their hind feet, and look you in the face, if you have fortitude enough to face them, they will turn and run off; but if you turn they will most assuredly tear you to pieces; furnishing strong proof of the fact, that no wild beast, however daring and ferocious, unless wounded, will attack the face of man.

On the morning of the 22d September we again renewed our tour, traveling at the rate of eight or ten miles a day; catching a few beaver, as we passed along—nothing strange occurring until the 30th, when we arrived at the foot of a great mountain, through which the river Laramies passes. We attempted to follow the river through the mountain, but we soon found this to be impossible, as the bluffs of huge rocks projecting several hundred feet high, closed in to the very current. We then turned down the side of the mountain, in search of a place to cross it. On the 1st day of October we came to a buffalo trail crossing the mountain, and after ascending to near the summit, we encamped for the night. About midnight it commenced snowing, and continued to fall so fast that we were obliged to remain there until the morning of the 4th, when we again renewed our

11

journey, and in the evening we arrived in the valley on the north or west side of the mountain. Here, finding no snow and beaver signs plenty, we deemed it advisable to remain a few days for the purpose of trapping, and the first night we caught twenty beaver. We remained here until the 12th, when we proceeded eight or ten miles further up the South Fork of the river, and again encamped for the purpose of trapping. On the 18th, finding beaver getting rather scarce, we proceeded a few miles further up the valley and encamped again.

This valley is supposed to be seventy or eighty miles long, and from ten to fifteen miles wide; and is enclosed on the one side by the main chain of the Rocky Mountains, and on the other by great piney hills, running out from the main body of the mountain, with the river Laramies passing through the center of it, the banks of which are covered with timber, from one-fourth to one-half a mile wide. Outside of this timber, the plain is completely smooth; and on a clear morning, by taking a view with a spyglass, you can see the different kinds of game that inhabit these plains, such as buffalo, bear, deer, elk, antelope, bighorn, wolves, &c. These plains are poor, sandy and level—the grass thin and short.

Oct. 22d. The nights getting somewhat cold, and snow falling more or less every day, we began to make preparations to return to our winter quarters, at the mouth of Laramies River; and on the 25th commenced our tour down the river. On the 28th we arrived at the mountain, that we crossed going up, but found it impossible, owing to the enormous depth of the snow to pass over it. On the morning of the 30th we started a number of men up and down the valley, in search of a place to cross the mountain, who returned the next day and reported that they had found no passing place over the mountain; when under these circumstances a majority of the company decided in favor of encamping in this valley for the winter, and when the ice melted out of the river, in the spring, commence trapping until such times as the snow melted off the mountain; when we would return to the mouth of the river, where we had secreted our goods.

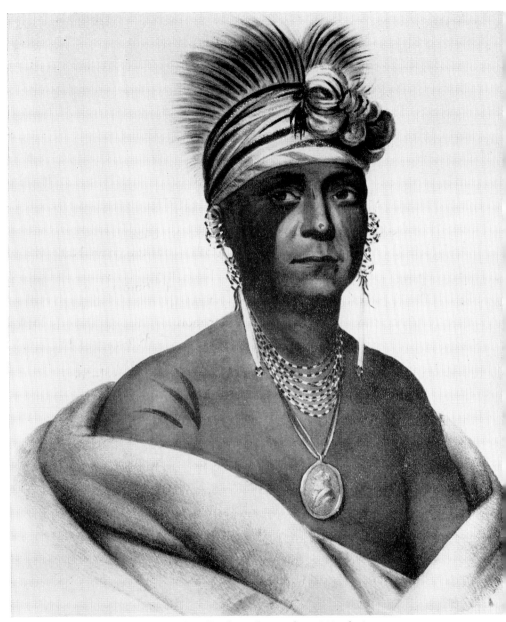

From McKenney and Hall, *The Indian Tribes of North America*

White Plume, the Kansa Chief, 1821

Chimney Rock

A Painting by Alfred Jacob Miller

On the 1st day of November, we commenced traveling up the valley, in search of a suitable place to pass the winter, and on the evening of the 4th, we arrived at a large grove of cottonwood timber, which we deemed suitable for encamping in. Several weeks were spent in building houses, stables, &c. necessary for ourselves and horses during the winter season.[9] This being done, we commenced killing buffalo, and hanging up the choice pieces to dry, so that if they should leave the valley we would have a sufficient quantity of meat to last us until spring. We also killed deer, bighorn sheep, elk, antelope, &c., and dressed the hides to make moccasins.

About the 1st of December, finding our horses getting very poor, we thought it necessary to commence feeding them on cottonwood bark; for which purpose each man turned out and pealed and collected a quantity of this bark, from the grove in which we were encamped for his horses; but to our utter surprise and discomfiture, on presenting it to them they would not eat it, and upon examining it by tasting, we found it to be the bitter, instead of the sweet cottonwood. Immediately upon finding we were deceived, men were dispatched up and down the valley, in search of sweet cottonwood, but returned without success.[10] Several weeks were spent in fruitless exertion to obtain feed for our horses; finally we were compelled to give it up, and agreed that our horses must all starve to death. The great depth of the snow, and the extreme coldness of the weather, soon prevented our horses from getting anything to subsist upon, and they commenced dying. It seldom happened during all our difficulties, that my sympathies were more sensibly touched, than on viewing these starving creatures. I would willingly have di-

[9] This winter camp was on the Laramie River, probably in south-central Albany County, Wyoming, west of the Laramie Range.
[10] Trappers learned from the Indians the value of the sweet cottonwood as a winter food for horses. William H. Ashley observed in 1826, "When the round leaf or sweet bark cottonwood can be had abundantly, horses may be wintered with but little inconvenience. They are fond of this bark, and, judging from feeding it to my horses last winter, I suppose it almost, if not quite as nutritious as timothy hay." H. C. Dale (ed.), *The Ashley-Smith Explorations and the Discovery of a Central Route to the Pacific, 1822–1829*, 138–39.

vided my provisions with my horses, if they would have eaten it.

On New Years Day, notwithstanding our horses were nearly all dead, as being fully satisfied that the few that were yet living must die soon, we concluded to have a feast in our best style; for which purpose we made preparation by sending out four of our best hunters, to get a choice piece of meat for the occasion. These men killed ten buffalo, from which they selected one of the fattest humps they could find and brought in, and after roasting it handsomely before the fire, we all seated ourselves upon the ground, encircling, what we there called a splendid repast to dine upon. Feasting sumptuously, cracking a few jokes, taking a few rounds with our rifles, and wishing heartily for some liquor, having none at that place, we spent the day.

The glorious 8th arrived, the recollection of the achievements of which are calculated to gladden the hearts of the American people; but it was not so glorious to us. We found our horses on that day, like Packenham's forces, well nigh defunct.[11] Here we were in this valley, surrounded on either side by insurmountable barriers of snow, with all our merchandise and nothing to pack it upon, but two mules—all the rest of our horses being dead. For ourselves we had plenty to eat, and were growing fat and uneasy;—but how we were to extricate ourselves from this perilous situation was a question of deep and absorbing interest to each individual. About the 10th we held a consultation, to decide what measures should be taken for our relief. Mr. Stephens, our pilot, having been at Santa Fe, in New Mexico, some eight or ten years previous, informed the company that horses in that place were very cheap; and that he was of the opinion he could take them to it, if they saw proper to follow him. It was finally agreed upon by the company that a part of them should start for Santa Fe; but not, however, without a good deal of confusion; as many were of the opinion that the snow on the mountain in the direction of Santa Fe would be found to be as insurmount-

[11] This was the anniversary of General Andrew Jackson's victory in the Battle of New Orleans, January 8, 1815, which was still an occasion for patriotic celebrations.

able as in the direction of their merchandise, and also that the distance was too great to attempt to travel on foot at that season of the year. It appearing from the maps to be little short of eight hundred miles.

On the morning of the 14th, finding everything in readiness for our Santa Fe trip, we set out, each man with his bedding, rifle and nine beaver skins, packed upon his back; leaving four men only to take care of our merchandise and the two mules. The beaver skins we took for the purpose of trading to the inhabitants of Santa Fe for horses, mules, &c. We appointed from the middle of April till the middle of May as our time for returning; and if we did not return within that time, our four men were to wait no longer, but return to the mouth of the Laramies River, to meet the rest of the company. We continued in the direction of Santa Fe, without any extraordinary occurrence, for several days—found game plenty and but little snow, until we arrived at the foot of a great mountain, which appeared to be totally covered with snow. Here we thought it advisable to kill and jirk some buffalo meat, to eat while crossing this mountain, after which we continued our course; finding much difficulty in traveling, owing to the stormy weather and deep snow—so much so indeed, that had it not been for a path made by the buffalo bulls it would have been impossible to travel.

The channel of the river where it passes through these mountains is quite narrow in places and the banks very steep. In such places the beaver build their dams from bank to bank; and when they become old the beaver leave them, and they break and overflow the ground, which then produces a kind of flag grass. In the fall of the year, the buffalo collect in such places to eat this grass, and when the snow falls too deep they retreat to the plains; and it was in these trails that we ascended the mountain.

We still continued our course along this buffalo path, which led us to the top of the mountain; nothing occurring more than it continued to snow day and night. On the 25th we arrived on the top of the mountain, and wishing to take a view of the country, if it should cease snowing. In the morning it still continued to snow so rapidly that we were obliged to remain in camp all day, and about the middle of the day, we ate the last of our jirk, and that evening we were obliged to go to bed supperless.

On the 29th it still continued to snow, and having nothing to eat, we thought it high time to be making some move for our preservation or we must perish in this lonely wilderness. The question then arose, shall we return to the valley from whence we came, or continue in the direction of Santa Fe. This question caused considerable disturbance. Those who were in favor of going ahead, argued that it was too far back to game—that it would be impossible to return before starving to death; while those who were for returning contended that it was the height of imprudence to proceed in the direction of Santa Fe. Accordingly we made preparations and started. We traveled across the summit of the mountains, where we found a plain about a mile wide, which with great difficulty, owing to the fierceness of the wind, we succeeded in crossing; but when we attempted to go into the timber, on the opposite side from the mountain, we found it impossible, in consequence of the depth of the snow, and were obliged to turn back and recross the plain. As we returned by the fire we had made going over the plain the first time, we halted for the purpose of mutually deciding what to do; when it was determined by the company that we would if possible, return to our four men and two mules. We then started in search of the buffalo path which we had followed to the top of the mountain; but owing to the strong wind, that had blew for several days, and the increased depth of the snow, it was invisible. We then attempted to travel in the snow without the path, but we found this equally as impossible, as in the direction of Santa Fe.

Here we were, in a desolate wilderness, uninhabited (at that season of the year) by even the hardy savage or wild beast—surrounded on either side by huge mountains of snow, without one mouthful to eat, save a few beaver skins—our eyes almost destroyed by the piercing wind, and our bodies at times almost buried by the flakes of snow which were driven before it. Oh! how heartily I wished myself at home; but wishing, in such a case appeared useless—action alone could save us. We had not even leather to make snowshoes, but as good fortune would have it, some of the men had the front part of their pantaloons lined with deer skin, and others had great coats of different kinds of skin, which we collected together to make snowshoes of. This appeared to present to us the only means of escape from starvation and death. After gathering up everything of leather kind that could be found, we got to making snowshoes, and by morning each man was furnished with a pair. But what were we to subsist upon while crossing the mountain was a painful question that agitated every bosom and employed every tongue in company. Provision, we had none of any description; having eaten everything we had that could be eat with the exception of a few beaver skins, and, after having fasted several days, to attempt to travel the distance of the valley without anything to eat, appeared almost worse than useless. Thinking, however, that we might as well perish one place as another, and that it was the best to make an exertion to save ourselves; and after each man had selected two of the best beaver skins to eat as he traveled along, we hung the remainder upon a tree, and started to try our fortune with the snowshoes. Owing to the softness of the snow, and the poor construction of our snowshoes, we soon found this to be a difficult and laborious mode of traveling. The first day after we started with our snowshoes we traveled but three or four miles and encamped for the night, which, for want of a good fire, we passed in the most distressing manner. Wood was plenty but we were unable to get it, and it kept one or two of the men busy to keep what little fire we had from going out as it melted the snow and sunk down. On the morning (30th Jan.) after roasting and eating some of our beaver skins, we continued our journey through the snow. In this way we continued to travel until the first day of February, in the afternoon, when we came to where the crust on the snow was sufficiently strong to carry us. Here we could travel somewhat faster, but at the best not

17

much faster than a man could crawl on his hands and feet, as some of the men from hunger and cold were almost insensible of their situation, and so weak that they could scarcely stand on their feet, much less walk at speed. As we approached the foot of the mountain the snow became softer and would not carry us. This caused the most resolute despair, as it was obviously impossible, owing to extreme weakness, for us to wade much farther through the snow. As we moved down the mountain plunging and falling through the snow, we approached a large spruce or cedar tree, the drooping branches of which had prevented the snow from falling to the ground about its trunk—here we halted to rest. While collected under the sheltering bows of this tree, viewing, with horrified feelings the wayworn and despairing countenances of each other, a Mr. Carter, a Virginian, who was probably the nighest exhausted of any of the company, burst into tears and said, "here I must die." This made a great impression upon the remainder of the company, and they all, with the exception of a Mr. Hockday and myself, despaired of going any further. Mr. Hockday, however, after some persuading, telling them that if they had strength to follow us we would break the road as far as possible, if not out to the valley, succeeded in getting them started once more. Mr. Hockaday was a large muscular man, as hardy as a mule and as resolute as a lion; yet kind and affectionate. He was then decidedly the stoutest man in the company, and myself, probably, the next stoutest. As for our captain, Mr. Stephens, he was amongst the weakest of the company.

We resumed our journey, and continued to crawl along through the deep snow slowly till the evening of the fourth, when we arrived in the plain at the foot of the mountain. Here we found the snow so shallow that we could dispense with the use of our snowshoes; and while in the act of taking them off some of the men discovered, at the distance of seventy or eighty yards; two animals feeding in the brush, which they supposed to be buffalo, but from blindness, caused by weakness and pine smoke, could not be positive. Mr. Hockday and I were selected to approach and kill one of the animals without regard to what they

18

might prove to be, while the remainder of the company were to go to a neighboring grove of timber and kindle a fire. Having used our guns as walking canes in the snow, we found them much out of order, and were obliged to draw out the old loads and put in new ones, before attempting to shoot. After taking every precaution we deemed necessary to insure success, we started and crawled along on our hands and knees, until we approached to within ten or fifteen steps of the animals, when Mr. Hockday prepared to shoot; but upon finding that he could not see the sight of the gun or hold it at arms length, forbore, and proposed to me to shoot. I accordingly fixed myself and pulled the trigger. My gun missed fire! I never was so wrecked with agitation as at that moment. "There," said I, "our game is gone, and we are not able to follow it much further"; but as good fortune had it, the buffalo (for such we had discovered them to be) did not see nor smell us, and after raising their heads out of the snow and looking around for a few moments for the cause of the noise, again commenced feeding. I then picked the flint of my gun, fired and broke the back of one of the buffalo, my ball not taking effect within eighteen inches of where I thought I aimed.—The men in the grove of timber, on hearing the report of my rifle came staggering forth to learn the result, and when they received the heart-cheering intelligence of success they raised a shout of joy. It was amusing to witness the conduct of some of the men on this occasion. Before we had caught the buffalo they appeared scarcely able to speak—but a moment after that, were able to hollow like Indians at war. I will not describe the scene that followed here—the reader may imagine it—an account of it would be repulsive and offensive rather than agreeable. This was the ninth day since we had eaten anything but dried beaver skins. We remained at this place four days feasting upon the carcass of this buffalo, during which time we recruited considerably in strength and spirits, and on the 8th we resumed our journey down the river in search of our four men and two mules, and soon landed in the valley where game was plenty, and but little snow to obstruct our march. We

19

continued our journey, killing plenty of game and living well, without any strange occurrence until the 14th, when we halted within a short distance of our old camp, and sent two or three of our worst looking men ahead to see whether they would be recognized by the four men. They were not known immediately on arriving at the camp, but no sooner engaged in conversation than they were recognized by the four men, and heartily welcomed back.

Here we remained at our old station until the 14th of March, during which period, having plenty of good buffalo meat to eat, we regained our usual health and appearance. Anxious to be doing something, eight of us made preparations to start again to Santa Fe for horses. We were to travel south, along the foot of the mountain till we came to a certain river which heads in the mountain near where we had hung the beaver skins on the pine tree; after finding this river we were to commence trapping, and also to endeavor to get the beaver fur off the mountain into the valley. The balance of the company, thirteen in number, were to remain at the camp and secrete the merchandise, and then follow us to this river, where we were to meet; and if we had succeeded in getting the beaver skins off the mountain, we were to join together and proceed in the direction of Santa Fe. With this understanding we started, and pursued our course slowly along the base of the mountain—found game plenty—met with no obstacle to impede our march, and on the 20th we arrived on the bank of the river. After remaining here a few days the ice melted out of the creeks and we commenced and continued to trap for beaver until the 28th, during which time we caught a fine quantity of fur and built ourselves a wigwam after the Indian fashion.[12] The weather continuing warm and pleasant, and having a large quantity of dried meat on hand, we concluded to hide our traps, beaver skins, baggage, &c., in our wigwam and pack a portion of the jirked meat on our backs and

---

[12] The reference is apparently to a temporary, conical structure of poles, branches, and bark set up by Indians of the Northern Plains on horse raiding and hunting expeditions and commonly referred to as a "war lodge."

make an effort to get the beaver skins off the pine tree where we had left them in January. We started, and after traveling up the river along the side of the mountain for two or three days, we came in contact with huge mountains of snow and insurmountable icebergs, and were compelled to abandon our course and return back again to the plain. When we had arrived within a short distance of our wigwam, on our return, we discovered several trails of moccasin tracks in the snow. Some of the company became somewhat alarmed at these signs, supposing them to be the trails of hostile Indians—others appeared rejoiced and said it was the remainder of our company. The dispute was soon decided, for on arriving at our wigwam, we found it completely robbed of everything we had left in it—traps, blankets, beaver skins and other utensils were all gone—nothing remained but the naked frame of the little hut. We had now nothing left to sleep on save one old blanket for each man which we had with us on the mountain, and had lost nearly all our traps. Under these highly aggravating circumstances some of the men became desperate, declared they would retake their property or die in the attempt. For my part, I viewed the matter calmly and seriously and determined to abide the dictates of prudence only. Seeing from the trail of the Indians that they were not very numerous, and had a number of horses with them, we determined, after some controversy, to rob them of their horses, or other property commensurate to our loss. Accordingly we made preparations for our perilous adventure—we ate supper, prepared our firearms, and a little after dark set out on search of the enemy—the night was calm and clear. We traversed the valley up and down for several hours without making any discoveries; we then ascended an adjacent hill, from the summit of which we discovered at a considerable distance a number of dim fires. A controversy here arose amongst the men as to the expediency of attacking the Indians. It was finally decided, however, by a majority of the company; that we should attack them at all hazards. We started in the direction of the fires, and after traveling some distance, and having lost sight of the fires, some of the men again became

21

discouraged, and strongly urged the propriety of abandoning the project; but on calling a vote a majority again decided in favor of attacking the Indians and in a few minutes we arrived on the top of a hill, within fifty or sixty yards of the enemy's camp. Here we halted for the purpose of reconnoitering. At this time the moon was just rising above the summit of the mountain, and casting its glimmering rays o'er the valley beneath, but did not shine on the Indian camp. There were five fires, and the Indians appearing more numerous than we had expected to find them, we thought it advisable to be as careful and judicious about attacking them as possible. At the foot of this hill, near a large rock, we left our hats, coats and everything that was unnecessary in action—we also designated this as a point of meeting, in case we should get separated in the skirmish; and had an understanding that but two should fire at a time, and that Captain Stephens was to command. Mr. Hockday and I were selected to shoot first. We then started and crawled silently along on our hands and knees until we got within eight or ten steps of one of the fires, where we laid down in the brush, with our heads close together to consult as to the most proper mode of surprising the savages, whose dusky forms were then extended in sleep around the dying embers. While in this position, some eager for the conflict, others trembling with fear, a large dog rose from one of the fires and commenced growling and barking in the most terrifying manner. The spell of silence was now broken, and an immediate and final skirmish with our enemy rendered unavoidable. Thinking ourselves rather too much exposed to the fire of the Indians we retreated fifteen to twenty steps down the bank. Some of the Indians then came to the top of the bank and commenced shooting arrows at us, and yelling at the extent of their lungs. At this moment Mr. Stephens was heard to say in a firm tone "now is the time my boys, we must fight or die," upon this Mr. Hockday and I fired; one of the Indians on the bank was seen to fall, and the remainder ran back to the camp. On hearing the report of our rifles the Indians, to the number of two or three hundred, rose out of the bushes and literally covered the plain, while their terrific war whoop—mingled with an occasional crack of a rifle, rendered the aspect of things more threatening than the most timid had before anticipated. We ran to our appointed place to meet, but before we had time to gather our baggage, we found ourselves completely surrounded and hemmed in on every side by the savages. Finding that we could not escape by flight, but must fight, we ran to the top of the hill, and having sheltered ourselves as well as we could amongst the rocks, commenced yelling and firing in turn (yelling is a very essential point in Indian warfare). This scene was kept up for near an hour without any damage to our company, and as we supposed, but little injury to the Indians. The savages seeing we were determined to defend ourselves to the last gave way on the opposite side of the hill from their camp, and we made our escape out of their circle, and were glad to get away with our lives, without any of our property or that of the Indians.[13] The scenes of this night will ever be indelibly impressed upon my memory.

After traveling five or six miles we came to a deep ravine or hollow—we carefully descended the precipice to the flat below, where we encamped for the night; but from fright, fatigue, cold and hunger, I could not sleep, and lay contemplating on the striking contrast between a night in the villages of Pennsylvania and one on the Rocky Mountains. In the latter, the plough-boy's whistle, the gambols of the children on the green, the lowing of the herds, and the deep tones of the evening bell, are unheard; not a sound strikes upon the ear, except perchance the distant howling of some wild beast, or war-whoop of the uncultivated savage—all was silent on this occasion save the muttering of a small brook as it wound its way through the deep cavities of the gulph down the mountain, and the gentle whispering of the breeze as it crept through the dark pine or cedar forest and sighed in melancholy accents; nor is it the retiring of the "god

[13] The enemy tribe cannot be identified with any degree of certainty. However, it is more probable that these Indians were Cheyennes or Arapahos than members of the treacherous Arikara Tribe.

of day" to his couch in the western horizon that brings on this desolate scene—his rising in the east does not change the gloomy aspect—night and day are nearly the same in this respect.

About midnight we were alarmed by a shrill whistle on the rocks above, and supposing it to be the Indians in pursuit of us we seized our guns and ran a few rods from our fires. After waiting for some time without hearing any more noise, one of the men ascended the precipice, and discovered that the object of our fears was a large drove of elk. In the morning we continued to travel down this ravine—and I was struck with the rough and picturesque appearance of the adjacent hills. On our right and left, arose like two perpendicular ramparts, to the height of near two hundred feet, two chains of mountains. Not a blade of grass, bush or plant was to be seen on these hard slopes—huge rocks detached from the main body, supported by the recumbent weight of other unseen rocks appeared in the act of falling, and presented a frightful appearance—nothing met the eye but an inexhaustible avalanche of rocks—somber, gray or black rocks. If Dante had designed to picture in one of his circles, the Hell of Stones, he might have taken this scene for his model. This is one scenery in the vicinity of the Rocky Mountains; and perhaps an hour's travel would present another of a very different character—one that the artist who designed to depict a beautiful and enchanting landscape would select for a model.

After traveling some fifteen or twenty miles, we came to the trail where the main body of the Indians with whom we had the skirmish the evening before had passed along. It was near a half a mile wide, and the snow was literally trodden into the earth. I have since understood from whites who had been in the habit of trading with this nation, prior to their declaration of hostilities against the whites, that they numbered from seven to eight hundred warriors. Alarmed at this formidable appearance of the hostile Indians, we mutually declined the idea of going to Santa Fee, and turned and traveled in the direction of the main body of our company.

We continued to travel day after day, with all possible speed

—occasionally killing a buffalo, a goat, or a bighorn, as we passed over the plains and prairies which were literally covered with these animals; and on the morning of the 9th of April, we arrived safe at our old camp, and were gratified to find our thirteen men and two mules in the enjoyment of good health, with plenty to eat and drink. After exchanging civilities all around, by a hearty shake of the hand, and taking some refreshment, which was immediately prepared for us, I related to the company the dismal tidings of the near approach of the hostile Indians, and the circumstances of being robbed by them, and being defeated in the attempt to retake our property. All were now satisfied of the imprudence of attempting to go to Santa Fe by the route, as well as of the necessity of devising some other method of saving our merchandise. We finally concluded to conceal our merchandise, baggage, fur, and everything that we could not pack on our backs or on the two mules, and return to our appointed winter quarters, at the mouth of the Laramies River, with the expectation of meeting Captain Gant, and obtaining some assistance from him. On the morning of the 20th of April, having made every necessary preparation, we set out on our journey for the mouth of the Laramies River. After two days' travel, we came to the foot of the mountain which we had endeavored in vain to cross in November. The snow was still deep on the top of it; but by aid of the buffalo trails, we were enabled to scale it without much difficulty, except that our mules suffered with hunger, having had nothing to eat but pine brush. At the foot of the mountain we found abundance of sweet cottonwood, and our mules being very fond of it, we detained two or three days to let them recruit from their suffering in crossing the mountains. This mountain and the one we left our fur on are covered with the most splendid timber of different kinds such as fir, cedar, white pine, &c. On the margin of the rivers and creeks in the plains, the only timber is cottonwood, undergrowth, willow, and rose bushes; out in the middle of the plains there is none of any description. In the month of June, a person by taking a view of the country east of this mountain with a spy glass, could see nothing but a level plain extending from the foot of the mountain as far as the eye can penetrate, covered with green grass, and beautiful flowers of various descriptions; and by turning to the northwest, the eye meets nothing but a rough and dismal looking mountain, covered with snow, and presenting all the appearance of dreary winter. These plains extend to the state of Missouri, with scarce a hill or a grove of timber to interrupt the sight, and literally covered with game of almost every kind.

On the 25th we again resumed our journey down the river, and continued ahead without any difficulty—passing over nearly the same ground that we had traveled over going up the fall before; killing plenty of game—buffalo, deer, bear, bighorn, antelope, &c., and on the 20th May we landed at the mouth of the Laramies; but to our utter astonishment and discomfiture we discovered that not one of the parties had returned according to agreement.

[*Here is the end of what was published before.*[14] *The manuscript continues as follows*:]

After remaining here until the 29th, our commander, Mr. Stephens, and another man took the two mules, which by this time had greatly recovered from their famished state, and started in search of the other parties. In vain they traveled up and down the La Platte and its tributaries, but no traces of the lost companions could be discovered, and on the 6th of June they returned, much fatigued and disheartened. During their travels they had discovered, on some of the creeks, sixty or seventy miles from our encampment, many signs of beaver—encountered several grizzly bears, and several times narrowly escaped the Indians; Mr. Stephens having had several balls shot through his clothes. In this situation we remained for five or six days, when Mr. Stephens proposed that each man should go on foot, with a trap or two on his back, his blankets, together with what we could pack upon the two mules, and commence trapping on these creeks. This proposition was objected to by some of the company

[14] This publisher's note in the original edition refers to the fact that the preceding portion of the book had been published in the *Clearfield Republican*.

who were in favor of securing some of Captain Gant's merchandise, find the Indians and purchase horses of them. So many different propositions were here made that nothing definite could be agreed upon. Mr. Smith, Mr. Fully and myself agreed to repair to the trapping ground and commence operations, with the understanding that Captain S., should receive a certain share of the profits, as a recompense for the discovery he had made. Accordingly having everything arranged, on the 11th we started, leaving the remainder of the company to pursue their own course.

Mr. Stephens having a part of the men indebted to him for clothing, &c., and knowing that if they remained at camp he would not be able to collect it, told them that if they would go and bring the beaver fur off the mountain, where we had left it in January last, he would ensure them an equal share of the proceeds of our trapping expedition—and they, with this understanding set out. This contract was made without any consultation having been had with us; and the men, not aware of anything but fairness on the part of Stephens in making this bargain, marched for the fur, and succeeded in getting it off the mountain into the plain, without much difficulty, packed it on their mules, together with what we had left in our winter cabins, and brought the whole to the mouth of the Laramies River. In the meantime, Smith, Fully, and myself were busily engaged in trapping on the tributary streams of the river Platte. We encountered much difficulty and danger in this excursion, from wild beasts and hostile Indians. One circumstance with a bear I must relate:—On a pleasant summer evening, when nothing seemed disposed to disturb the tranquility of our forest home, we built a fire under the cliff of a large rock, on the bank of a small creek, to roast some buffalo meat. After having cooked and eat our evening repast, I was standing close to the rock, apart from the other men ten or twelve feet—all at once one of them jumped up and ran off, exclaiming "the bear," "the bear!" I instantly cast my eyes to the top of the precipice, where they encountered this hideous monster seated on the rock with his mouth wide

27

open, and his eyes sparkling like fire. My whole frame shook with agitation. I knew that to attempt to run would be certain death. My gun was standing against a tree within my reach, and after calling for the aid of my companions, I raised my rifle to my face and taking deliberate aim at the most fatal spot, fired—which brought sir Bruin to the ground. In the meantime Smith and Fully came to my assistance, and also discharged the contents of their rifles into his head.

In a few days afterwards we were joined by the rest of the company, who, having secreted the fur, &c., at the mouth of the Laramies River, had come in search of us. We now, for the first time, got a knowledge of the conduct of Stephens relative to our fur. The men informed us of the contract between them and Stephens. We answered that we could agree to no such contract—that the fur belonged to us, and that we intended to keep it. They then devised other means to secure their share of 150 beaver skins (the whole number we had caught). Stephens then told the men that he would not be accountable for any of the fur, and the only way to obtain any of it, was to take it by force. Seeing the folly of further resistance—18 against 3— we were obliged to surrender our earnings, which they took and divided equally among themselves.

The next day we left this company at whose hands we had received such ill treatment, and returned to the mouth of the Laramies, with the expectation of meeting Captain Gant—but we were sadly mistaken—on our arrival there no traces of Capt. G.'s company could be discovered.[15] Next day Mr. Stephens and his party also returned. After remaining here three days together, hunting, fishing, and indulging in other amusements, Mr. Fitzpatrick and a company of 115 men, came to our camp. He was

[15] Leonard's party had had no news from Captain Gantt since they left him to ascend the Laramie the previous September. However, W. A. Ferris at the rendezvous in Pierre's Hole in June, 1832, learned from a party of trappers who had made their hunt to the southward that they "saw Captain Ghantt [sic], at the head of fifty or sixty men, on Green River; he had procured horses from the Spaniards of New Mexico, and had made his hunt on the sources of the Arkansas, and tributaries of Green River, without molestation by the Indians." Paul C. Phillips (ed.) *Life in the Rocky Mountains*, 150-51.

Trapping Beaver in the Mountains

A Painting by Alfred Jacob Miller

War Ground

A Painting by Alfred Jacob Miller

on his way to join his company on the west side of the mountains, on the Columbia River, and to supply them with merchandise, ammunition, horses, &c. This company informed us that the firm of Gant & Blackwell had become insolvent. At this news we all became discouraged; and finally Mr. Stephens and the whole company agreed to join in with Fitzpatrick and go with him to his rendezvous, where we were to make arrangements as to hiring, purchasing equipments, &c. Mr. Stephens took 120 beaver skins which belonged to Captain Gant, and sold them to Fitzpatrick, which he secreted in the ground, with the intention of raising them when on his return to Missouri—in consideration of which, he was to furnish him with horses and such other equipments as he might want.

July 1st. Having made this arrangement with Mr. F., our camp was all confusion at an early hour this morning, preparing to depart for the Columbia River.[16] Mr. F., took one of the fleetest and most hardy horses in his train, and set out in advance of the main body, in order to discover the disposition of the various Indian tribes through whose dominions we were to travel, and to meet us at a designated point on the head of the Columbia River. After packing up all our movable property, we started in the course which he had taken with a force of near 150 strong, many of whom were afraid of nothing, and anxious to meet any danger. We this day traveled about twenty miles and encamped for the night. The weather was serene and warm, and the men all in high spirits, as we had plenty of fresh meat.

July 2d. Early in the morning we resumed our journey—stopped in the heat of the day to rest our horses—country quite beautiful—soil rather poor, abounding with sand plains. Traveled about fifteen or twenty miles and encamped for the night.

July 3d. This day we made but little progress in traveling in consequence of a heavy fall of rain—came in contact with a large drove of buffalo, out of which our hunters succeeded in

[16] Leonard's dates for his movements in the summer of 1832 are faulty. The party must have left the mouth of the Laramie before the middle of June. His reference to the Columbia River alluded to the entire system of that great river from the headwaters of the Snake River to the Pacific Ocean.

killing ten—one of the men received a bite from a snake, but as it was not of a very poisonous species, the wound soon healed and the victim was more scared than hurt—but little variation in the scenery of the country.

July 5, 6 & 7. The weather was fair—traveled at the rate of twenty-five miles per day—nothing of interest occurred. The country through which we passed is rather rough, abounding with game of every description, and is remarkable for the plentitude of wild goats. I have seen the plains literally covered with them. Occasionally the men would fall to and kill them by hundreds. We also fell in with a party of Indians, but on their seeing our forces, fled, without attempting to injure us. We were unable to ascertain the name of the tribe to which they belonged.

July 8th. Early in the morning we resumed our journey, but had not proceeded far until we found ourselves in the midst of a bed of quicksand. So deep was the sand in some places that several of our horses were completely swamped in it, and it was with great difficulty that we succeeded in getting round this swamp, as it were, to continue our journey. Having surmounted this difficulty, one of our men, a Mr. White, who wandered from the company, came well nigh falling a victim to the fury of a grizzly bear—having in the encounter had one of his arms literally torn from his body, and had it not been for the timely assistance rendered by some of his companions, who afterwards killed the bear, his death would have been the inevitable consequence. This night we selected a high piece of ground for our encampment, where the wind continued to assail us most violently during the whole night. The next day we traveled about twenty miles, without meeting with anything of consequence.

July 10th. Finding that we were making but little headway in our traveling, we resolved to increase our speed, and accordingly the whole company was on the move at an early hour this morning. We found our route beginning to grow still more obstructed by rocky cliffs, which are dispersed over this section of the mountain region for many miles, and present an appearance to the beholder similar to a meadow covered with hay-cocks.

As the country continued to grow rough, game became scarce, and we began to kill such meat as we *could,* and not such as we *chose;* indeed we thought ourselves very fortunate when one of our hunters would succeed in killing a goat or an antelope—species of meat which we would not look at, when in the vicinity of deer and buffalo. This part of the mountain is covered with beautiful timber of the best quality, such as fir, cedar, &c. We only traveled about ten miles this day. On the following morning we resumed our journey, and continued to travel day after day, when, after a long and toilsome voyage, we arrived at the point on the Columbia River, designated to meet Mr. Fitzpatrick. Judge of our surprise, when on arriving here no traces of him could be discovered. In vain we searched for some clue to this, to us, melancholy circumstance. What can detain him? was the question asked by each of us. Disappointment is heart-sickening under any circumstance, but to be disappointed under such circumstances, and in such a place, was perplexing in the extreme. One scouting party after another were despatched to gather some tidings of the lost Fitzpatrick, but all to no purpose. Had he been destroyed by the savages? The former brilliant success of the man's intercourse with the Indians would not warrant such a belief, as he had many times previously passed over these mountains with no other companion than his trusty steed. The most natural conclusion at which to arrive was that the dull and cloudy weather had caused him to lose his course, and that he had become bewildered and was yet wandering through the wilderness.

After a fruitless search of several days, we concluded to descend the river and search for the company which Mr. Fitzpatrick had left there the summer before, where we had a faint hope that we might find Mr. F. in safety. The first day we traveled about twenty miles and encamped for the night on the bank of the river. Although we knew that we were in the vicinity of the savage Blackfeet Indians, yet but few traces of them had been discovered through the day, and we therefore retired to rest in our encampment without taking the necessary precautions for defense, in case of an attack. But it was not long before we were enabled to appreciate the consequence of our negligence, or fancied security. About midnight we were awoke from our slumbers by a furious attack by a large party of Blackfeet. They fired into our tents before we were aware of their approach. Immediately each man was on his feet, and on the lookout. After a small skirmish of random shooting, which lasted an hour or so, the Indians, finding the strength of our forces, thought it best to retire from the field, with the loss of three killed, and as we supposed, eight or ten wounded. The loss on our side was one man wounded in the leg, five horses killed, three wounded, and fourteen stolen. The Blackfeet are a powerful nation and are better supplied with implements of war than almost any other tribe of this region.[17] They have always retained a most inveterate hostility to the Flatheads, against whom they wage a continual warfare, having at one time greatly reduced their strength, and on several occasions came well nigh exterminating the entire tribe. Of late years the Flatheads have been better prepared for war and have bravely held their own. This undying hostility appears to be owing to the Blackfeet refusing to let the Flatheads hunt buffalo on the east side of the mountain.

The following morning we took up our march and continued down the river. As we traveled along we seen many fresh signs of Indians, and apprehended much danger from them, which caused us to labor under the most intense fear lest we should fall into an ambush of this crafty tribe. We killed several fat deer, goats, and an antelope, and encamped on a high hill, from which we had a beautiful view of the surrounding country; where we could see the different kinds of game traversing the plains at leisure, contented, and undisturbed, save when aroused from their lair by the sudden onset of the Indian hunter. This

[17] The Blackfeet had made peace with the American Fur Company in 1831 and had begun peaceful trade with that firm at the mouth of the Marias River (Fort Piegan) that summer. However, the Blackfeet distinguished between those traders and the trappers who took beaver without any compensation to the Indians. Their hostility toward trappers was as great as ever.

night we very prudently stationed a strong guard round our encampment, and were permitted to pass the night in peace, which was quite warm and pleasant. In the morning we resumed our journey, and about the middle of the day found ourselves in the vicinity of another tribe of Indians. We sent a flag to their camp, which was received in the most friendly manner. This proved to be the Flathead tribe. These Indians are more pacific and pleasing in their manners than any tribe we had yet encountered, and reside mostly on the river of that name. I will here quote the description of this tribe as given by Mr. Cox, a gentleman well acquainted with the Indian character, which fully embraces my own views:—"The Flatheads have fewer failings than any tribe I ever met with. They are honest in their dealings—brave in the field—quiet and amiable to their chiefs—fond of cleanliness, and are decided enemies to falsehood of every description. The women are excellent wives and mothers, and their character for fidelity is so well established that we never heard of one single instance of one proving unfaithful to her husband. They are remarkably well made—rather tall—slender, and never corpulent."[18] The Flatheads are well accustomed to the manners and customs of the white race, and in many respects appear ambitious to follow their example. Some years ago, they were in the habit of using a process to flatten the heads of their children, which they deemed a very essential addition to their appearance; but since they have had intercourse with the whites they have abandoned this abominable practice. The process of flattening the head is this:—Soon after the birth of the infant, it is placed in a kind of trough and a piece of bark fastened by means of strings through the trough, and pressed hard upon the forepart of the head, which causes it to grow flat. In this painful position they are kept a year, and in some instances over a year. They are very hospitable to strangers, and are tried friends of the white people. On coming to their village a white person al-

[18] Ross Cox, North West Company trader, wintered among the Flatheads in 1813–1814 and wrote a description of the life of those Indians, from which this brief quotation is taken. See Ross Cox (Edgar I. Stewart, ed.), *The Columbia River*, 135.

ways receives the best to eat, drink and smoke, and are always ready to pilot the traveler through their country. In the summer season this tribe live in the buffalo country on the head of the Columbia River, where they never fail to come in contact with their cold-hearted enemies, the Blackfeet, who are the most ferocious and unsparing enemy of the white men, because the Flatheads have been supplied by the whites with munitions of war. In the fall the Flatheads again return to the plains, and in the winter subsist on salmon, roots and small game. They are always well supplied with horses, and when provision becomes scarce in one section, they pack all they have upon the backs of their horses, and remove to another. Their houses are made of slim pine poles from twenty to thirty feet long, twelve or fifteen feet apart at the bottom, and joined together at the top, forming a structure in the shape of the roof of a common dwelling house. These are covered with dressed buffalo skins sewed together. A fire is built in the middle of the cabin, and its shape forms a kind of flue or draft for the smoke—rendering this simple structure quite a comfortable habitation at the most inclement season of the year. No storm can affect them, nor no cold can reach their inmates. When moving camp these poles are taken down and one end fastened to the sides of the mule or horse and the other end dragging on the ground forming a sort of dray. The infants are put into a sack or bag, made of leather, which closes on one side by strings; this is fastened to a board near three feet long and one wide, where they are kept constantly, with the exception of an occasional dressing, &c., until a year old. To the back of this board they have a cord attached, by which they hang the sack to the saddle, whilst traveling.[19]

After remaining here two days to observe their manners, customs, and mode of living, and getting all the information we

[19] Leonard's first-hand knowledge of the Flatheads was exceedingly limited. His description of head deformation refers to the practices of the Chinook near the mouth of the Columbia. There is no evidence that the Flatheads (Salish) ever deformed their heads. Their summer and winter buffalo hunts were conducted east of the Rockies around the headwaters of the Missouri and not "on the head of the Columbia River" as Leonard stated.

desired, we resumed our journey, taking one of the Indians to pilot us to the station of Mr. Fitzpatrick's company. After several days tedious and toilsome traveling, and no extraordinary occurrence, we joined the company on the 2nd of August.[20] It was with feelings of peculiar delight that we here beheld the visages of white men, who were no less pleased to give us a welcome reception. But a melancholy gloom was visible in every countenance, when we discovered that Fitzpatrick had not arrived. Great excitement prevailed, and vigorous measures were immediately taken to rescue him, if he had not before this, as many supposed, fallen a victim to the enraged fury of the merciless savage or the ravenous appetite of some ferocious beast of prey. Small companies were despatched in various directions on the tributary streams of the Columbia. Diligent search was kept up for some time without success, and our search was about to be abandoned as fruitless; and indeed some of the parties had give up in despair, and returned to camp, when, a party, who had wandered into the vicinity of the Blackfeet Indians, were reconnoitering their movements in a valley from a high bluff, saw, and immediately recognized, Fitzpatrick's horse, with which the Indians were running races. Was this calculated to inspire hope? or was it not rather an omen that our employer was destroyed by these Indians. Vigilant search was made to make further discoveries; and to the great joy of every man, he was a length found on the banks of the Pieres River, which forms a junction with the Columbia, near the rendezvous of Fitzpatrick's company. When found he was completely exhausted, and so much wasted in flesh, and deformed in dress, that, under other circumstances, he would not have been recognized. The poor man was reduced to a skeleton, and was almost senseless. When his deliverers spoke of taking him to camp, he scarcely seemed to comprehend their meaning. After eating some dried buffalo meat, and a little maize, he grew better, and placing him

[20] Actually the caravan of William L. Sublette, with which Leonard traveled westward from the mouth of the Laramie via South Pass, reached the rendezvous site on July 8, 1832. Hiram M. Chittenden, *The American Fur Trade of the Far West*, I, 297.

35

on a horse, he was safely conveyed to camp. A general rejoicing ensued, for his appearance among us again was like that of one risen from the dead. Although I was not much attached to the man, for I could not banish from my mind the craftiness evinced by him when we first met with him on the east side of the mountains, yet I can scarcely describe my feelings of joy on beholding him safely returned. After resting a few days, and being nourished by the provender our camp would afford, he became able to relate the misfortunes which befell him in crossing the mountain, which I will give in his own words, as follows:

Adventures of Fitzpatrick

"For three or four days after I left the company I traveled without any difficulty, and at great speed, but the fourth and fifth, the weather being dull and cloudy, I got strayed from my course, and soon found myself in the midst of a rough hilly country, abounding with large loose rocks which some places almost prevented me from passing at all, and covered with various kinds of timber of the most magnificent description. In passing the nights in these solitudes my rest was constantly disturbed by the dismal howl of the wolf and the fierce growl of the bear—which animals were very numerous and would frequently approach within a few steps and threaten to devour me. One day after a toilsome ride, I dismounted, turned my horse loose to graze and seated myself on a rock, with the little remaining provision I had, to refresh myself. While thus seated resting my wearied limbs, and satisfying the gnawings of hunger, I was suddenly startled by a scrambling on the rocks immediately in my rear. I turned round and beheld a huge bear approaching me in double quick time. I instantly sprang to my feet, for I was well acquainted with his mode of warfare. I turned and faced his lordship, when he approached within about six feet of me, rose on his hind feet and most impudently stared me right in the face, for more than a minute. After discovering that I was

36

no ways bashful, he bowed, turned and run—I did the same, and made for my horse. Bruin was not so easy fooled; he seen my retreat and gave chase. I thought I could reach my horse and mount before the bear could reach me, but the approach of the bear frightened my beast, and just as I was going to mount he sprang loose and threw me on the broad of my back. The bear was at my heels, and I thought that all chance of escape was now gone. Instantly I was again on my feet—and, as it were, in a fit of desperation, rushed towards the bear, which, fearing, as they do, the *face* of man, again turned and run. Sir Bruin stopped to secure the little morsel I had been eating, and retired a few paces to devour it. While the bear was thus employed, I crept to my gun, keeping the rock between him and me, having reached it, took deliberate aim and killed him dead on the spot. Having secured my horse, I fell to work at the carcase of my vanquished foe, and, after cooking and eating a choice piece of his flesh, left the rest to feed his kindred. It being now near night, I traveled two or three miles further and encamped for the night. The next morning appeared more favorable overhead, and I made an early start. Being on the banks of a small creek, I concluded to follow it awhile. After winding my way through the rocks and trees, till near the middle of the day, I came to a valley which seemed to be hemmed in on every side by huge towering hills. I had not traveled far in this valley before I found myself ushered into the presence of a hostile tribe of Indians. I halted to devise some means to effect a return without being discovered; but I soon found that it was too late. Immediately in my rear was a choice set of young warriors—in front, and on both sides by high and craggy mountains. My noble steed than him, I would defy the whole Indian world to produce a stouter, swifter, or better, was now brought to the test. He started with the velocity of the reindeer, bounding over ditches, stones, logs and brush. Soon I began to ascend the mountain, but found it much too steep and rough. The Indians dismounted and followed on foot. I applied the whip, but in vain. My horse was compelled to yield to exhausted nature—and I dismounted and left my much

37

prized animal to fall a prey to the savages. I ran up the mountain with all possible speed, but finding that I must eventually be overtaken, I secreted myself in a hole among the rocks and closed the mouth of it with leaves and sticks. After remaining a few minutes in this subterranean cavern, I heard the ferocious yells of triumph of my pursuers, as they captured my lamented horse. The victory was not yet complete, although the horse was the principal prize. Some of them followed on and came close to my hiding place, passed and re-passed within reach without discovering me. What a moment of intense anxiety was this! All chance of escape cut off. No prospect of mercy if taken! Hope began to die—and death inevitable seemed to be the very next incident that would occur. They continued their search until near sunset, for they knew that I had not reached the summit of the mountain. As they retired down the mountain, squads of four or five would frequently halt and hold a busy consultation —then suddenly return to complete their search, as if they feared that some hollow tree or rocky cavern might escape unexplored. Finally, they gave me up in despair, and retired into the valley, with my horse.

"Now that I had escaped this scrutinizing search, I began to breathe more free and easy; but I was yet far from being out of danger. I was conscious that I had lost the course to the Columbia River, and could not tell how to regain it, even if I should succeed in escaping from my present perilous situation. I remained secreted in the rocks till long after dark, when I crawled out and surveyed the country as well as the darkness of the night would permit, and finally started in the direction which I thought I would have the least chance of meeting the Indians. I had not traveled far, however, until I was again doomed to be disappointed, for I was on the very borders of their encampment. Happily the camp was all quiet, and I returned quietly to my hiding place on the mountain, hoping that on the morrow I would be able to make some new discovery by which to extricate myself from these savages—which I judged to be the merciless Blackfeet. Early in the morning of the next day the hunt was resumed with increased vigilance; but again returned with disappointment. After the sound of their voices no longer reached me, I crawled to the mouth of the hole from which I presently beheld them running races with the horse they had taken from me. In this sport they spent the day. This village did not appear to be their permanent residence, but was handsomely situated on the banks of a small creek, and I suppose they had came here on a sporting expedition. The second night I made another effort to save myself, and gradually descended the mountain to the creek some distance below the camp. This I followed, until daylight again compelled me to hide myself; which I did by crawling into the brush close to the creek, where I secreted myself till darkness again gave me an opportunity to resume my journey. During the day I seen a number of the Indians pass and repass up and down the valley, whom I supposed to be hunters. This day I again had a view of my horse under the saddle of the chief of the tribe, as I supposed; but did not attempt to rescue him. The following night I traveled a short distance down the creek when I came to where it empties into the Pieres River. Here I came to my reckoning of the country, and thought that if I could escape from hunger and beasts of prey, I could manage to elude the Indians. Supposing that the Indians were not so numerous on the opposite side of the river, I resolved to cross over—for which purpose I built a raft of old logs, laid my shot-pouch, gun, blanket, &c. on it, and pushed for the opposite shore. After getting nearly across, the current became very rapid, and I began to descend the river at a rapid rate until I struck a rock which tore my frail craft to pieces— committing myself, gun, blanket and all to the watery element. Being weak from hunger and exertion, it was with great difficulty that I succeeded in reaching the land, with the loss of my only companion, and my only hope in this wilderness of dangers— my gun. I stood on the bank in the midst of despair. I had no other weapon than a butcher knife to fight my way through a country swarming with savages and equally dangerous wild beasts. On my knife depended all hope of preventing starvation.

39

The loss of my blanket was also severe, as the weather was sometimes quite cold, and I had no other clothing than a shirt and vest—having thrown the rest away when pursued by the Indians on the mountain. I followed the banks of this river for two days, subsisting upon buds, roots, weeds, &c. On the second evening whilst digging for a sweet kind of root, in a swamp, I was alarmed by the growl of wolves, which were descending the hill to the river, about fifty yards distant. The only chance of escape now, was to climb a tree, which I did immediately. Here I was compelled to roost until daylight, in the most painful agitation. The wolves tearing up the ground and gnawing at the tree so that I sometimes feared they would cut it through. The third day I traveled with great speed, not even stopping for anything to eat. On the fourth I happened where the wolves had killed a buffalo. Here I satisfied my appetite by collecting all the meat that was left on the bones, made a fire by rubbing two sticks together, and cooked it. From the gluttonous fill which I took of this meat, I was enabled to travel three or four days, without any particular occurrence; but I found that the further I descended the river, the scarcer became the roots, buds, &c., on which I must depend for subsistence, and I was finally obliged to turn my attention to get something to eat, without traveling any further. For several days I loitered about from place to place, but could find no nourishment. My body began to grow weaker and weaker, until I was no longer able to walk. Still my mind held its sway, and I was well aware how desperate was my situation. Finally losing all prospect of getting anything more to eat, and no hope of being found by my companions or friendly Indians, I thought of preparing myself for death and committed my soul to the Almighty. I have no recollection of any thing that occurred after this, until I found myself in the hands of my deliverers."[21]

[21] This account, which purports to tell the story in Fitzpatrick's own words, has been quoted many times. Fitzpatrick's biographers, LeRoy R. Hafen and W. J. Ghent, acknowledged their indebtedness to Leonard as the basis for their description of this hair-turning adventure. See their *Broken Hand*, 94–96, 298. However, the hostile Indians encountered were not Blackfeet but Gros Ventres,

The story of Fitzpatrick created much excitement in our camp. Some were determined on immediately chastising the Indians and retaking his horse. Others, who were not friendly disposed towards Mr. F., would not credit his story. For my part I thought the man had related nothing more than the truth as to his sufferings, for nothing less could have reduced him to the condition in which he was found. In a few days all was restored to order and tranquility, and we commenced making arrangements for trapping, &c.

The Columbia is a strong, clear and beautiful river at this point (the junction of the Lewis River) and is about one thousand yards wide. The Wallah Wallah empties into it about fourteen miles lower down—which is rather muddy, and a very rapid stream.[22] There was at this rendezvous at this time, about four hundred white people, who lived in constant intercourse with the Flatheads and "Nez Perces," or Pierced Nose tribes, which latter consists of one thousand warriors, besides women and children, and live in the closest friendship with their neighbors, the Flatheads. They are said to act honorable in all their dealings, nor do they now practice treachery and stealing so extensively as most of the tribes below this; although, when first discovered by the whites, a *brave* was esteemed according to his success in stealing. They have now reformed, and a white man can at all times find a trusty friend in a Nez Perces.[23]

Among the discoveries of importance which we made here was nine of Captain Gant's men, who had left us at the mouth of

political allies of the Blackfeet who shared their inveterate enmity toward the trappers.

[22] Leonard's editor appears to have had little knowledge of the geography of the Columbia River system. This description refers to the mouth of the Snake River in the present state of Washington. The rendezvous of 1832 was actually held in Pierre's Hole (or Valley) on one of the headwaters of the Snake (or Lewis River) known as Pierre's or Teton River, located westward of present Grand Teton National Park in Wyoming.

[23] The Nez Percés from the Middle Columbia Valley were common participants in the rendezvous of the mountain men. They had met the Flatheads, Shoshonis, and Crows in annual trading fairs in this general region before the days of the white men's mountain fur trade. See Francis Haines, *The Nez Percés*, for a history of this tribe.

the Laramies. In crossing the mountain they had several encounters with the Indians, and finally lost their horses and three of their men. After traveling about for a number of days, under the direction of a Mr. Saunders, their leader, they came across a party belonging to this rendezvous, whom they followed, and had arrived at camp a few days before us. No important arrangement was made among the men with regard to trapping, &c., until the people gathered in from the different parts of the mountain. In the meantime fifteen of us joined together, each man furnishing an equal quantity of merchandise, horses, &c., and to receive an equal share of the proceeds.[24]

August 25th. Everything necessary for our expedition being ready this morning, we started in a southern direction, but did not go far until we encamped for the night—thinking that if we had neglected anything which we would stand in need of, we would thus discover it. The next morning finding all things in order, we continued traveling down what is called Pieres Hole, or Valley. This valley is situated on the river of the same name, and is from seventy to eighty miles in length, with a high mountain on the east and west—each so high that it is impossible to pass over them, and is from eight to ten miles wide. The river runs immediately through the center, with a beautiful grove of timber along either bank; from this timber to the mountain, a distance of four or five miles, there is nothing but a smooth plain. This meadow or prairie is so perfectly level that a person may look up or down as far as the eye will reach without meeting anything to obstruct the sight, until the earth and sky appear to meet. After traveling a few miles this morning, some of the men, in taking a view of the country before us, discovered something like people upon horses, who appeared to be coming toward us. After continuing in the same direction for some time we came in view with the naked eye, when we halted. They advanced towards us displaying a British flag. This we could not compre-

---

[24] Having heard nothing from their employers, Gantt and Blackwell, since early the previous fall, these men thus organized their own partnership as free agents.

hend; but on coming closer discovered them to be hostile Indians. We immediately despatched a messenger back to the rendezvous for reinforcements and prepared ourselves for defense.
The Indians commenced building a fort in the timber on the
bank of the river; but at the time we were not aware of what
they were doing. After waiting here a few hours we were re-
inforced by two hundred whites, two hundred Flatheads, and
three hundred Nez Perces Indians. The Indians with the British
flag, on seeing such a number of people galloping down the plain
at full speed, immediately retreated within their fort, whither
they were hotly pursued. The friendly Indians soon discovered
them to belong to the Blackfeet tribe, who are decidedly the most
numerous and warlike tribe in the mountains, and for this reason are not disposed to have any friendly intercourse with any
other nation of an inferior number, unless they are good warriors
and well armed with guns, &c. We thought we could rush right
on them and drive them out of the brush into the plain and
have a decisive battle at once. We advanced with all possible
speed, and a full determination of success, until we discovered
their fort by receiving a most destructive fire from the enclos-
ure. This throwed our ranks into complete confusion, and we all
retreated into the plain, with the loss of five whites, eight Flatheads and ten Nez Perces Indians killed, besides a large number
of whites and Indians wounded. The formation of their fort astonished all hands. We had been within a few hundred yards of
them all day and did not discover that they were building it.
It was large enough to contain five hundred warriors; and built
strong enough to resist almost any attempt we might make to
force it. After dressing the wounded, and having reconnoitered
their fort, our forces were divided into several detachments, and
sent in different directions with the intention of surrounding the
fort and making them prisoners. This was done under the super-
intendence of Fitzpatrick, who acted as commander-in-chief.

In a case of this kind any man not evincing the greatest degree of courage and every symptom of bravery, is treated as a
coward; and the person who advances first, furthest and fastest,

and makes the greatest display of animal courage, soon rises in the estimation of his companions. Accordingly with the hope of gaining a little *glory* while an opportunity offered, though not for any electioneering purpose, as a politician in the States would do—I started into the brush, in company with two acquaintances (Smith and Kean) and two Indians. We made a circuitous route and came towards the fort from a direction which we thought we would be least expected. We advanced closer and closer, crawling upon our hands and knees, with the intention of giving them a *select* shot; and when within about forty yards of their breastwork, one of our Indians was shot dead. At this we all lay still for some time, but Smith's foot happening to shake the weeds as he was laying on his belly, was shot through. I advanced a little further, but finding the balls to pass too quick and close, concluded to retreat. When I turned, I found that my companions had deserted me. In passing by, Smith asked me to carry him out, which met my approbation precisely, for I was glad to get out of this unpleasant situation under any pretext—provided my reputation for courage would not be questioned. After getting him on my back, still crawling on my hands and knees, I came across Kean, lying near where the first Indian fell, who was mortally wounded and died soon after. I carried Smith to a place of safety and then returned to the siege. A continual fire was kept up, doing more or less execution on both sides until late in the afternoon, when we advanced to close quarters, having nothing but the thickness of their breastwork between us, and having them completely surrounded on all sides to prevent any escaping. This position we maintained until sunset, in the meantime having made preparations to set fire to the fort, which was built principally of old dry logs, as soon as night would set in, and stationed men at the point where we thought they would be most likely to make the first break, for the purpose of taking them on the wing, in their flight. Having made all these preparations, which were to put an end to all further molestation on the part of the Blackfeet, our whole scheme and contemplated victory was frustrated by a most ingenious and well executed

44

device of the enemy. A few minutes before the torch was to be applied, our captives commenced the most tremendous yells and shouts of triumph, and menaces of defiance, which seemed to move heaven and earth. Quick as thought a report spread through all quarters, that the plain was covered with Blackfeet Indians coming to reinforce the besieged. So complete was the consternation in our ranks, created by this stratagem, that in five minutes afterward there was not a single white man, Flat-head, or Nez Perces Indian within a hundred yards of the fort. Every man thought only of his own security and run for life without ever looking round, which would at once have convinced him of his folly. In a short time it was ascertained that it was only a stratagem, and our men began to collect together where our baggage was. I never shall forget the scene here exhibited. The rage of some was unbounded, and approached to madness. For my own part, although I felt much regret at the result after so much toil and danger, yet I could not but give the savages credit for the skill they displayed in preserving their lives, at the very moment when desperation, as we thought, had seized the mind of each of them.

By the time we were made sensible of the full extent of our needless alarm, it had began to get dark; and on ascertaining the extent of the injury which we received (having lost 32 killed, principally Indians), it was determined not to again attempt to surround the fort, which was a sore disappointment to some of the men who were keen for chastising the Indians for their trick.[25] We then took up our march for the rendezvous; but on

25 This was the Battle of Pierre's Hole, the most famous of the many Indian fights in which the mountain men engaged. It was fought on July 18, 1832. The Indian enemies were Gros Ventres, not Blackfeet. A number of the other partici-pants in and eye-witnesses of this conflict have described it. Among them were Nathaniel J. Wyeth (F. G. Young, ed.), *The Correspondence and Journals of Captain Nathaniel J. Wyeth, 1831–1836*, 158–59), John B. Wyeth (Oregon: *A Short History of a Long Journey*, 63), William L. Sublette (Letter in *Missouri Republican*, October 16, 1832); George Nidever (William H. Ellison, ed., *The Life and Adventures of George Nidever, 1802–1883*, 26–30), and Louis Rivet (Montana Historical Society Contributions, X, 252). W. A. Ferris not only de-scribed the battle but also the appearance of the Indian's fortifications when he revisited the battlefield in the following spring. (Paul C. Phillips, ed., *Life in the*

starting one of our party of fifteen men, who had first started out
the day before, could not be found. Search was made, and he
was found in the brush, severely wounded. After carrying him
on a litter a few miles he died and was buried in the Indian style:
which is by digging a hole in the ground, wrapping a blanket
or skin round the body, placing it in the hole, and covering it
with poles and earth. This is the manner of interring the dead
in this country both by the Indians and whites, except in the
winter season on account of the ground being frozen, when the
Indians are in the habit of wrapping their dead in buffalo robes
and laying them on poles from one tree to another, on which
poles the corpse is tied with cords.

The next morning we raised another war party and went back
to the battle ground, but no Indians could be found. They must
have left the fort in great haste for we found 42 head of horses,
together with Fitzpatrick's which they had taken on the mountain, two warriors and one squaw lying dead inside of their fort,
besides a large quantity of their baggage, such as furs, skins,
&c. There must have been a great number of them, from the
holes they had dug in the ground around their dead horses and
the edges of the fort, say from three to four hundred. I learned
afterwards that the Nez Perces Indians shortly after found seven
more dead Blackfeet in some brush close by, where they had
been secreted to save their scalps, which is the principal object
with these Indians, in order to have their women dance. In the
afternoon we returned to the rendezvous and presented Mr.
Fitzpatrick with his long-lost and highly valued horse, which
seemed to compensate for all the sufferings and hardships which
he had encountered.

After remaining here a few days a violent dispute arose between Stephens and Fitzpatrick about the price of the horses
which the latter was to give to the former for the beaver skins
of Gant's which Stephens had sold to Fitzpatrick. No person

Rocky Mountains, 154–55, 201–202). The most comprehensive account of this
conflict appears in Washington Irving's, *The Adventures of Captain Bonneville,
U.S.A., in the Rocky Mountains and the Far West*, 88–98.

interfered, for we all knew that it was a dishonest transaction from beginning to end. Fitzpatrick having everything in his own possession, was therefore contented and as independent as any mean man who had it in his power to make his own terms. Stephens, on the contrary, was in a bad situation—having paid beforehand, and not being able to force measures, had to put up with what he could get. Finally he succeeded in hiring four men, and started back to the mouth of the Laramies to secure the fur which he had sold to Fitzpatrick. He had not left many days, however, until he was overtaken by a scouting party of those Indians we had surrounded in the fort. Two of his men were killed, and himself shot through the thigh—having the two mules along, which was the balance of the original stock, one of which was killed, and the other brought back the wounded Stephens, who died in a few days afterwards from mortification taking place in the wounded leg.

A few days after this occurrence, we were visited by a party belonging to the Nor-West, or British Trading Company,[26] from whom we were enabled to learn the way the Blackfeet Indians had got possession and fought under the British flag. It appeared by their story that these Indians some months previous had fell on a party belonging to their company—but few of whom escaped to tell the fate of their comrades—and among the spoils which they obtained was this flag, which they used as a signal to deceive and mislead their enemies, whom they might meet in these extensive plains.

September 1st. After remaining here until today, during which time Mr. Saunders joined our company of fifteen, which made up for the one that was killed, and who was the only one besides myself of Captain Gant's company; leaving the balance with Fitzpatrick—some hiring with their equipments which they purchased on credit. We set to work making preparation to start the following morning on our second attempt to reach some region where we could prosecute our business of trapping to

26 The reference is to the Hudson's Bay Company, which had absorbed the North West Company of Montreal in 1821.

some advantage. The conditions of our agreement were the same as on the first expedition, viz:—each man to find an equal portion of traps, guns, and ammunition and to receive an equal share of the peltries which we might catch.

On the morning of the 2nd September, having everything ready, we left the rendezvous, all in a fine humor. We arrived on the headwaters of the Multenemough River without anything of moment occurring—where we made our fall's hunt. After traveling near one hundred miles southwest from the top of the mountains, or from the head of Lewis River, we got totally out of the range of the buffalo.[27] We were told by the natives that those animals were never known further west, which is something singular, as the country is just the same, if not better as to grass. These Indians subsist principally upon salmon, and such other fish as they can catch, with the assistance of roots, buds, berries, and some small game, which they kill with the bow and arrow. They are generally of a more swarthy nature, small and cowardly, and travel in small gangs of from four to five families—this they are compelled to do in order to keep from starvation. They are always roving from plain to plain, and from valley to valley—never remaining in one place longer than till game gets scarce. When on the move the women have to perform the most laborious part—having charge of the transportation of their baggage. While doing this, a female, the most feeble of their sex, will carry a load of perhaps a hundred weight a whole day without manifesting the least fatigue or complaint. This tribe, which I believe is called the Bawnack, or Shoshonies, are the most indolent and have the least ambition of any tribe we had yet discovered. They are lazy and dirty; and only strive to get as much as will keep them from starving. They are no way ill disposed towards the whites, or at least they never disturbed us—with the exception of stealing a few of our traps. We continued moving down the Multenemough for several hundred

[27] Again Leonard's geography is confusing. The Multnomah was the Willamette River of western Oregon. Leonard's party appears to have traveled southward from Pierre's Hole into present Nevada, west of Great Salt Lake, to the Humboldt or to the Owyhee River.

miles, during which time we subsisted principally upon beaver, deer, and bighorn—though we still had a little jirked buffalo meat. Between trapping and trading we had made quite a profitable hunt. To get a beaver skin from these Indians worth eight or ten dollars, never cost more than an awl, a fish-hook, a knife, a string of beads, or something equally as trifling.

As winter was approaching, we began to make arrangements to return to some more favorable climate, by collecting our fur and giving each man his share of the baggage. We traveled back with great speed, and arrived in the buffalo country on the first of November, where we met with a nation of Snake Indians, with whom we made some small trades for buffalo robes and skins for the winter. The manners and customs of the Snake Indians are very similar to those of the Flatheads, with the exception of stealing, which they consider no harm. The Snake Indians, or as some call them, the Shoshonies, were once a powerful nation, possessing a glorious hunting ground on the east side of the mountains; but they, like the Flatheads, have been almost annihilated by the revengeful Blackfeet, who, being supplied with firearms were enabled to defeat all Indian opposition. Their nation has been entirely broken up and scattered throughout all this wild region. The Shoshonies are a branch of the once powerful Snake tribe, as are also the more abject and forlorn tribe of Shuckers, or more generally termed, Diggers and Root-Eaters, who keep in the most retired recesses of the mountains and streams, subsisting on the most unwholesome food, and living the most like animals of any race of beings.[28]

We left the Snake Indians and took a more southern direction to the Bear River, which empties into Big Salt Lake—followed

[28] The identification of the many tribes of Shoshonean-speaking Indians seen by Leonard west of the Rockies between the summer of 1832 and that of 1834 is not possible on the basis of his fragmentary descriptions. Generally the Shoshonis and Bannocks of Idaho and Wyoming were distinguished from the host of Paiute tribes farther south and west by the fact that the former tribes possessed horses while the latter did not. The dispossession of the Shoshonis from the plains of the Upper Missouri by the Blackfeet armed with firearms was accomplished prior to 1800.

this river for two days, and then crossed over to Weabers River.[29] These two rivers are about the same size, say from two to three hundred yards wide, and from three to four hundred miles long. They run south parallel with each other, and empty into the Big Salt Lake on the north side, at no great distance apart. This lake is much larger than any other west of the mountains—supposed to be two hundred miles long, and near the same in width. It is surrounded on the north, about the mouths of the rivers, by a mountainous and broken country, and on the south and west by a barren, sandy plain, in a manner incapable of vegetation. There is also a hill or peak near the center of it so high that the snow remains on it the greater part of the year. The water is of such a brackish nature that only part of it freezes in the coldest weather of the winter season. Its briny substance prevents all vegetation within a considerable distance of the margin of the lake. The Bear and Weabers rivers are the principal streams by which it is fed. In the spring of the year, when the snow and ice melts and runs down off the mountains, this lake rises very high, on account of it having no outlet; and in the fall, or latter part of the summer, it sinks—leaving salt one and two inches thick on some parts of its shores. It is situated on the west side of the mountains, between the waters of the Columbia and Rio Colorado, or Red River, and is called by the natives the Great Salt Lake. The rivers which empty into this lake abound with many kinds of fish, such as trout, catfish, and others suitable for hook and line, particularly at their mouths. Where the country is low, and small streams empty into them, the dams of the beaver cause the water to overflow its banks, and makes a swampy, marshy country for miles round. People trapping on these streams are compelled to construct canoes of bull and buffalo skins in order to visit their traps.

On leaving this lake we continued our journey towards the headwaters of the Colorado, which stream empties into the Gulf of California. After a tedious but not unpleasant tramp of several

---

[29] Bear River flows into Salt Lake from the north; Weber River, which flows northwest, empties into Salt Lake on the east side.

days we came to a beautiful situation on one of the main feeders of this river, where we halted to make preparations to spend the winter—it now being about the middle of November. We had remained here but a few days, during which time we were occupied in building tents, &c., for winter, when we were visited by a party of seventy or eighty Indian warriors. These Indians manifested the best of friendship towards us while in our camp and said they were going to war with the Snake Indians—whose country we were now in—and they also said they belonged to the Crow Nation on the east side of the mountains. In all the intercourse had with them while they were with us, not the least symptom of deception was discovered, and they parted with us manifesting as much regret as if we had been old acquaintances. But we were doomed to experience the faith of the Crow Nation—for, on the same night of their departure, they returned and stole five of our best hunting horses. This was a serious loss to us and a valuable prize for them—for an Indian belonging to these hunting and warring tribes is poor indeed if he is not the owner of a horse, as it is upon this animal they much depend for success in chasing the buffalo, and upon him greatly depends the fate of the battle.

Having a man in our company who had once been a captive in their village, and who could talk and understand a little of their language, we resolved at all hazards to give chase and retake our horses. We steered across the mountains towards the southern headwaters of the Missouri River. The first stream we came to on the east side is called Bighorn River—down which stream we traveled for some days, until we came to their village situated at the mouth of Stinking River.[30] In this village we found a Negro man, who informed us that he first came to this country with Lewis and Clark—with whom he also returned to the state of Missouri, and in a few years returned again with a Mr. Mackinney, a trader on the Missouri River, and has remained here ever since—which is about ten or twelve years. He

[30] The Stinking (or Stinkingwater) River of the traders is now named the Shoshone River, which enters the Bighorn in extreme north-central Wyoming.

has acquired a correct knowledge of their manner of living, and speaks their language fluently. He has rose to be quite a considerable character, or chief, in their village; at least he assumes all the dignities of a chief, for he has four wives with whom he lives alternately. This is the custom of many of the chiefs.[31]

After informing the Negro of our stolen horses, he told us that they had them, and that the reason they were taken from us was because we were found in their enemies' country, and that they supposed we were going to trade them guns, &c. By giving the chiefs some trifling presents our horses were produced in as good trim as when they left us. (I shall say nothing more of these Indians at present, as I shall have occasion to speak of them when I again visit their village.)

About the first of January 1833, the game getting scarce in this vicinity, the Indians left us and moved down the river. We remained at this station employing our time in hunting, fishing, and such other sports as we could come at, but without any particular occurrence, until the 20th of February, when we set out on our spring hunt. We crossed the country to the river Platte without any difficulty, and continued down this stream to the junction of it and the Laramies, where we had joined Fitzpatrick's company in the previous spring, and where also we had parted with Captain Gant. On encamping for the night we found a tree off which the bark was pealed, and wrote on with a coal, that, by searching in a certain place mentioned, we would find a letter—which we did and found the document, written in Gant's hand, which stated that only two parties had returned, viz:— Washburn's and his own—and also that Captain Blackwell had come up from the States with a supply of provision, merchandise, ammunition, &c. The letter went on to detail the hardships, sufferings, and misfortunes which they had encountered, which

---

[31] This was not Captain William Clark's servant, York, but the mulatto, Edward Rose, who went up the Missouri with Manuel Lisa in 1807 and remained among the Crows to become a leader of influence among that tribe. In 1823 he was with Ashley in the battle at the Arikara villages, and thereafter assisted Ashley's trappers in the Crow country. He served as interpreter at the first treaty between the United States and the Crow Indians at the Mandan villages in 1825.

only amounted to this: that they had lost their horses last winter and had been to Santa Fe and purchased more—while crossing the mountain his party had accidentally met with Washburn and his company—that they then ascertained for the first that the company was insolvent and had declined doing business in this country—and that they [Gant's party] had left this place in September last to go and establish a trading post on the Arkansas River with the Arapahee Indians. The letter closed by stating that Stephens' party had left him and joined Fitzpatrick. This letter was directed to Mr. Saunders, who was in our company, and who, Gant supposed, would be the first to return.

Soon after the contents of the letter were made known to the company, some men were sent across the Laramies River to see if they could make any discoveries of importance, as we could see the remains of what we supposed to be an old encampment on its banks. These men, after searching for some time, found where several buffalo had been slaughtered, and from the manner in which it was done it was evident that it was the work of a party of hostile Indians—and not being able to trace which direction they had steered, we were at a great loss to know what to do—having no person to act as commander. There was much difference of opinion and great contention about which way we should take. Our object was, if possible, to avoid meeting with the Indians, as our force was small and not well prepared to encounter a band of savages defended with firearms. Finally, it was decided that we should leave the rivers and strike for the mountains—thinking this route the least dangerous. After traveling an hour or so, we suddenly met with a body of eight or ten on horseback, who we judged to be hunting—not being backward about meeting with such a number, we marched boldly towards them. On this they immediately galloped off under full speed, in the direction which we were going. Thinking the main body to be in that direction, we thought to avoid them by turning to the right and keeping near the river. We did not advance far in this direction, however, until we suddenly came upon their encampment. Being thus led into their stronghold

53

by mere accident, we held a hurried consultation as to our own safety. Their horses and white lodges could be distinctly seen although we were some distance off, and we flattered ourselves that we had not yet been discovered by any in the village, and that we might yet escape. With this hope we sounded a retreat and marched slowly and silently back for the purpose of sheltering ourselves with the timber, where we intended to build a fort immediately, for we knew that even if we were not discovered now, the party we first met would give the alarm and the chase would be commenced. In going along, juking from bluff to bluff, in order to avoid being seen, we were overtaken by a single Indian on horseback. He would ride up at full gallop within twenty or thirty steps of us, and then suddenly wheel, ride back towards the camp, and then return as before. After repeating this several times, some of our men, when he came close, raised their guns, and he, thinking there might be danger in running away, came to us and told us that the chief had sent for us to come to his tent, to eat, smoke, and be friendly. Not having confidence in his good intentions, all declined the invitation, but told the messenger that we would just retire into the timber (where we intended to be occupied in the meantime in building a fort) and that if the chief wished to have anything to say to us, he could come there—for which we started into the woods, taking this fellow with us, with the intention of keeping him until the fort would be erected.

After going but a short distance our prisoner broke loose and immediately ran onto some rising ground, where he made his horse perform many singular feats as a signal for his followers. We galloped off as fast as we could, but were soon surrounded on all sides, without anything to shelter us, except a hole formed by the sinking of water—which are very numerous in some of these plains. Into this hole we drove our horses, and expected to reach the top in time to keep the Indians at bay, and make peace with them. Before we got our horses properly secured in this hole there was hundreds of red men standing above and eagerly looking down upon us, uttering the most terrifying yells of vengeance, brandishing their guns, bows, and spears as if they would devour us. We were in just such a situation now as is calculated to bring on despair, with all its horrifying feelings, each man holding his gun cocked and ready, resolved to sell his life only with the last drop of blood. We stood in this situation, for a few minutes, waiting for them to commence, when there was one rushed into their ranks apparently much excited, who on addressing a few words to the warriors, they all put down their arms and made signs to us to come out, that they would not molest us. This we did, but it was with a watchful, jealous eye. The man whose timely arrival seemed to have put a stop to their designs, and who doubtless here saved our lives, now came forward and signified to us that we had better go with them to their camp, and eat, drink, and smoke, and he would exert his influence not to have us hurt—which advice we accordingly followed—taking our horses with us. On arriving at their camp, we found two who could talk the Crow language. The Rickarees (the nation in whose hands we now were) on being at war with the Crow nation took these two prisoners, as they told us, and adopted them as their brethren.[32] After manifesting a desire to be friendly with them, by smoking, &c. these Crow prisoners informed us that, had it not been for the timely arrival of the chief, when we were in the hole, we would most certainly have been cut to pieces. This is altogether probable. The feelings of every individual, as well as those of myself, when surrounded in this hole, were horrible in the extreme. The thought struck me, as I leaned against a rock, that here I must end my career. Our feelings may be imagined, but not described.

The Crow prisoners told as that the only reason they knew why the chief had interceded for us, was because he had not

[32] Pressure from the hostile Sioux, coupled with crop failure and scarcity of buffalo, had forced the Arikaras to abandon their earth-lodge villages on the Missouri in the fall of 1832, to become nomadic hunters in the valley of the Platte, from the forks to the mountains. They did not return to the Missouri to resume their former life as a semi-sedentary farming tribe until the spring of 1837. Edwin T. Denig, "Of the Arickaras," Missouri Historical Society Bulletin, Vol. VI, No. 2, 212–13, notes 26, 27.

previously been consulted on the subject (having been absent when we were discovered in the plain). This chief took a particular liking for us, and seemed determined to save us from the destructive vengeance of his people. He prepared a comfortable lodge for our own accommodation, in which we slept and eat. We remained in this situation two days and part of the third night, without anything to disturb us—during which time the Crow prisoners had many questions to ask about their own people. They appeared to be well treated, but notwithstanding they were anxious to make their escape. About midnight of the third night, our friendly chief, who slept with us every night, awoke us all, and told us the horrors of our situation. He said that he had a great many bad men among his followers, and that he was unable to appease their angry nature much longer—the red man thirsts for blood—that he had succeeded in saving us thus far, through much exertion—and that now, as the whole village was wrapt in slumber, it would be a fit time for us to escape. He gave us strict orders to travel with all speed and not to slacken our pace for two days and nights, for he said as soon as our departure would be known, we would be pursued. When our horses were brought out and all things was ready, we were escorted by the chief until daylight, when he left us and returned—manifesting the most intense anxiety for our safety. Indeed we were loth to part with this kind man, for we felt as if we were indebted to him for our lives. After parting with the chief, we pursued our journey with great speed, until the evening of the second day, when we were obliged to stop by a snow storm, which threatened us with destruction. We here turned our panting horses loose to graze and made preparations to pass the night—which we did undisturbed. In the morning, two of the horses were not to be found. All search was in vain, and we gave them up for lost—concluding that they had fell into the hands of our enemies, and if so, we had better be on the move, as they were doubtless close at hand; but the owner, not being satisfied, again started out. This detained us a while longer, when, apprehending danger from the Indians, we fired two guns as a signal for him that we were going, if he was yet in hearing. We resumed our journey, and after traveling a few miles, halted for the straggler—but he never returned.

The Rickarees are a powerful nation, consisting of about one thousand warriors. Their principal chief is called Highbacked Wolf.[33] Some twelve or fifteen years since, they were very friendly with the whites. This friendship was interrupted by the following circumstance:—About eight or ten years since, Mr. Mackenzie* took a chief from three different nations (one of which was a Rickaree) to Washington City, and while taking them back to their native wilds through Virginia, the Rickaree chief took sick and died in the city of Richmond. Mackenzie returned with the other two, Asnaboin and Mandan. While passing the Rickaree village (which was then situated on the Missouri River, from whence they have since removed to this country) Mackenzie stopped and informed them of the fate of their chief—which they disbelieved, and immediately declared war against the whites. They were much enraged and made a violent attack upon the boats containing the merchandise of Mr. Mackenzie—a great part of which they destroyed, and have since been the cause of the death of numbers of white men.[34]

* This name has heretofore been printed *Mackinney*—by mistake.—Pub.

[33] The principal chief of the Arikaras at that time was Bloody Hand (or Claws), whose portrait George Catlin painted from life in 1832. Highbacked Wolf was a principal chief of the Cheyennes of the same period. The Indians who captured Leonard and his companions may have been Cheyennes rather than Arikaras. Not only did the Cheyennes frequent the Laramie Valley, but they were at war with the Crows in the early 1830's.

[34] We do not know the source of Leonard's information regarding this delegation to Washington, but it appears to be a composite of facts relating to two or more such delegations. In 1806 an Arikara chief did visit Washington, and died there. (Dorothy Wollon [ed.], "Sir Augustus J. Foster and the 'Wild Natives of the Woods,' 1805–1807," *William and Mary Quarterly*, Vol. IX, No. 2, (1952), 207–208.) In 1807 Ensign Nathaniel Pryor attempted to escort a Mandan chief, Shahaka, who also had visited Washington, up the Missouri to his home. But the Arikaras, then at war with the Mandans, opened fire on the boats and refused to let them pass their villages. (Chittenden, *The American Fur Trade of the Far West*, I, 120–24.) In the years 1831–32, while Kenneth McKenzie was in charge of the American Fur Company's trading post of Fort Union at the mouth of the Yellowstone, a delegation of Indians from that region, which included The Light, son of an Assiniboin chief, was escorted to Washington

April 10th. Having lost all hope of being rejoined by our lost man, who we concluded had been captured by the Indians, we resumed our journey with fourteen men. Beaver we found in abundance—catching more or less every day, and everything seemed to promise a profitable business, until the 7th day of May —a day which will ever be remembered by each of us. Having encamped the night previous on a small creek in the Black Hills,[35] or on the headwaters of the river Platte, without timber or anything to shelter ourselves in case of an attack by the Indians, within eighty or one hundred yards. We this evening again turned our horses loose to graze, which is not by any means customary and much less prudent, while traveling through a country infested with hostile savages, as they are always hovering around the encampment, ready to lay hands on anything which they fancy. But on the present occasion we thought ourselves secure, as we had not seen nor met with any Indians for several days. On the following morning our horses were in sight on a hill a little above the encampment. About 9 o'clock three of us started to bring them down preparatory to our start. As there was no danger apprehended, neither of us took our guns. When we got to the top of the hill the horses were not to be seen— having descended the hill on the other side. The other two men soon found their horses and started with them to camp. After searching awhile I found mine with several others. The horses appeared much frightened, and I began to apprehend some danger. Whilst leading my horse towards the camp, an Indian, armed with a bow and arrow, came rushing upon me. I made several attempts to mount, but as often failed, for as I would spring to get on he would jump from under me. The savage now approached within about fifteen steps of me and signified that he would slay me unless I stopped and delivered up my horse.

by Major Sanford, Indian Agent for the Upper Missouri tribes. (John C. Ewers, "When the Light Shone in Washington," *Montana, the Magazine of Western History*, Vol. VI, No. 4, (1956), 2–11.

[35] The headwaters region of the North Platte was sometimes referred to as the Black Hills by trappers and early overland emigrants. This reference obviously is not to the Black Hills of South Dakota.

I sprang behind a bunch of bushes, which afforded me a tolerable shelter. He then made signs to me that if I would deliver myself up he would not hurt me. But this I refused. My only weapon was a large knife, which I carried in a scabbard at my waist. I drew this out and proposed to meet him. He then gave me to understand, that if I would lay down the knife he would lay down the bow and arrow, and we would meet and be friends. This I also refused to do. He made use of various inducements to get me from behind the bush, but I heeded them not, for I knew his intention was to kill me if it was in his power. He still advanced slowly toward me. I had been in several dangerous situations with the Indians and wild beasts, in some of which I had almost despaired. But none seemed to cause the same feeling as did my present predicament. Alone and unarmed—my situation was distressing indeed. I had no chance of escaping, and an immediate and cruel death I knew would be my fate if I surrendered. Whilst reflecting on what to do, and looking at him through an aperture in the bush, he shot an arrow at me, which fortunately missed its aim, and struck a branch within a few inches of my face, and fell harmless to the ground. By this time he had got quite close and being below me on the hill side, the thought struck me that I might despatch him with a stone— for which purpose I stooped down to get one, and carelessly let my body move from the shelter afforded by the bush, and at that instant I felt the pointed arrow pierce my side. I jirked the weapon out immediately, and started to run, still holding to my horse. I expected every moment as I ran quartering past the Indian to receive another, which I most certainly would have done, if the savage had been in possession of any more; and to run to the brush for those he had already discharged at me, would only be giving me time to escape. He then pursued me. After running a short distance I thought that my horse might be the means of saving my life, if I would leave him for the Indian, and accordingly I released my hold; but the Indian disregarded the horse and followed me. By this time, owing to the loss of blood from my wound, and the great excitement I was under,

59

I began to grow weak and faint, for I thought that every moment would be my last, as I heard the Indian puffing and blowing in my rear. We were now within sight of our camp, and were fortunately discovered by the men then there, who immediately ran to my relief. When I seen the face of my companions, I lost all my strength and fell prostrate to the ground. The Indian, foiled in his design on my life, retreated for the purpose of making sure of my horse, but in this he was also mistaken, for in turn he was pursued by my companions as hotly as he had chased me. When my mind again resumed its sway, I found myself in the camp carefully attended by my companions.

On entering into conversation with my companions, I found that I was not the only one who had encountered the Indians. I was ignorant of any more Indians being in the neighborhood than the one above alluded to, but it appeared by their story that, when the two men who started out with me were returning with the horses, they came across a large body of Indians, supposed to be about two hundred, who, after a sharp engagement, in which one of our men, named Gillam, of Illinois, was killed, and two wounded, succeeded in taking all our horses except two. Whilst I was listening to this lamentable story, our spies came running to the camp, bringing the unwelcome tidings that the Indians were again approaching with great speed, determined to ride over us. Each man now gathered a robe, blanket, guns, and such things as he could not do without, and carried the wounded into the brush at the foot of the hill, where we immediately commenced building a fort. The Indians approached and surrounded our encampment very cautiously, thinking that they would take us by surprise and capture man, beast and baggage without any difficulty—but they were outrageous when they found that there was nobody at home. They made the best of their victory however, and took everything we had left. When they had completed the pillage, which was only done when they could no longer find anything on which to lay their hands, they started off with their booty. After they had traveled some distance they halted and collected in a circle,

Trappers' Rendezvous

A Painting by Alfred Jacob Miller

Captain Walker and His Squaw

A Painting by Alfred Jacob Miller

within plain view of where we were, and smoked to the Sun, or Great Spirit. While going through this ceremony, some of them happened to discover us. On this, they quit smoking, left their horses and came on foot within thirty or forty steps of us, but on seeing our fort, which was only partly built, they turned away and left us, without making any attack. We remained in this situation until morning—those who were able being occupied in completing our fort. Soon after daylight the Indians again made their appearance and approached within a stone's throw of the fort, and on reconnoitering our situation they concluded that we were too well defended for them to gain any advantage over us—and the second time they left us without giving us a chance of trying our strength.

This morning I felt very weak and feeble from my wound, and began to fear that it was more serious than was at first supposed. About 10 o'clock the company was ready for the move, and I was packed between two horses. After traveling two or three miles we halted to rest near some brush—but not without having sentinels stationed for the purpose of keeping a vigilant look-out, for we still expected an attack from the Indians. Not long after we halted, our sentinels informed us that the savages were again approaching. We immediately went into the brush and commenced throwing up a fort. They this time approached very cautiously and seemed determined to put an end to our lives. When they observed that we were defended by a breast-work, they halted, reconnoitered on every side, and finally gave up and left us. These Indians who had hung round our path so long, robbed us of so much necessary property, killed one and wounded three of us, and came so nigh exterminating our whole company, we found out, belonged to the Rickaree Tribe—the same who frightened us in the sink hole on Platte River.

It was now that we had leisure to contemplate our situation. Some of us had labored hard, encountered one danger only to be eclipsed by another. We had at times endured the most excruciating suffering from hunger and fatigue—living in constant communion with the terrors of a wilderness studded with savages and no less dangerous beasts of prey, for two long years, and now left destitute of everything except an old greasy blanket, a rifle, and a few loads of ammunition, some thousands of miles from our paternal homes. To reflect on our present situation was enough to fill every heart with all the horrors of remorse. In fact, we felt a disposition about this time to do that which would not have been right, had an opportunity afforded. When we first embarked in this business, it was with the expectation that to ensure a fortune in the fur trade only required a little persever-ance and industry. We were not told that we were to be con-stantly annoyed by the Indians, but that it only required the observance of a peaceful disposition on our part, to secure their friendship and even support. Some of the Indians with whom we had intercourse, it is true, had been of great advantage to us in our trapping expeditions; but then it would be of short duration—for, if they would not render themselves obnoxious by their own treachery, our friendship with them would be sure to meet with an interruption through some ingenious artifice of a neighboring jealous tribe. Such had been the life we had led, and such the reward.

Our situation was not at all suited for sober calculation. Some appeared altogether careless what would become of them—seem-ing to have a willingness to turn in with and live the life of a savage, some two or three were anxious to leave the wilderness and return to the States as empty as when we left them. But this was rejected by nearly all, for we still had a distant hope of hav-ing better luck.

Some of our men were acquainted with the situation of the rendezvous of a company of traders on the headwaters of the Colorado, trading under the firm name of B. L. E. Bowville, & Co. and it was proposed to start for this post immediately.[36] After

[36] Captain Benjamin Louis Eulalie de Bonneville was born in France, April 14, 1796. He was graduated from West Point in 1815. While on frontier service at Fort Gibson he conceived the idea of requesting permission to take leave to conduct explorations in the Far West. With funds supplied by New York capital-ists, he embarked upon a venture in the fur trade, leaving Fort Osage in com-mand of a well-equipped party of 110 men, some of whom were experienced

much debate and persuasion, it was agreed that we should make the attempt. We got everything ready—the wounded having entirely recovered—and started on our long and tedious journey. As we traveled along we killed plenty of various kinds of game—met with nothing to interrupt our journey, and on the 25th of July arrived at the camp of Bowville, which at this time consisted of 105 men, together with a small company belonging to Mackenzie, from the Missouri River, of 60 men. We were well received by these men, most of whom had been in the woods for several years and experienced many hardships and privations, similar to what we had suffered. They seemed to sympathize with us about our loss, and all appeared anxious that we should turn in with them and restore our lost fortunes. After we had become thoroughly rested from the fatigue of our long tramp to this post, most of our men hired in different ways with this company. These men had been engaged in trapping in the vicinity of this rendezvous for a long time, and had caught nearly all the beaver, and were thinking about moving to some other section of country. There was a large tract of land laying to the southwest of this, extending to the Columbia River on the north, and to the Pacific Ocean and Gulf of California on the west and south, which was said to abound with beaver and otherwise suited as a trading country. As our company was now very large, the officers concluded on dividing it into three divisions. Accordingly Captain Bowville was left here with a considerable force to watch the movements of the Indians, and to do what he could

hunters and trappers, in May, 1832, bound for the Rocky Mountains. Although his three years in the fur trade were a failure financially, Bonneville returned east with a wealth of interesting experiences which he imparted to the famous writer, Washington Irving. Irving's work, first published under the title *The Rocky Mountains: or Scenes, Incidents, and Adventures in the Far West; from the Journal of Captain Benjamin L. E. Bonneville of the Army of the United States*, in 1837, brought to Bonneville a greater measure of fame as an explorer than was his due. Although Bonneville had overstayed his leave in the West, he succeeded in being reinstated in the army. He commanded the Gila River expedition against the Apaches in 1857, and from 1858 to 1861 commanded the Department of New Mexico. Bonneville died at Fort Smith, Arkansas, June 12, 1878. The extinct glacial lake which once covered the northwestern portion of present Utah, and a great dam on the Columbia River have been named in his honor.

at trapping, as this had been a great harbor for beaver, it was thought that there might be still some more to be caught. A Mr. Cerren with a few men was sent back to St. Louis, with four thousand pounds of beaver fur, with instructions to return and meet Captain Bowville at the Great Salt Lake in the following summer, with a supply of provisions to do the company for the two following years.[37] The other division, under the command of a Mr. Walker, was ordered to steer through an unknown country, towards the Pacific, and if he did not find beaver, he should return to the Great S. L. in the following summer. Mr. Walker was a man well calculated to undertake a business of this kind. He was well hardened to the hardships of the wilderness—understood the character of the Indians very well—was kind and affable to his men, but at the same time at liberty to command without giving offence—and to explore unknown regions was his chief delight.[38] I was anxious to go to the coast

[37] Michael Sylvestre Cerré, one of Bonneville's two experienced assistants, was born at St. Louis, April 17, 1803. He was a member of an old St. Louis family, prominent in the fur trade. In his youth he made one or more trips to Santa Fe. For one or two years prior to 1830 he was a member of the firm of P. D. Papin and Company, which operated Teton Post on the Missouri below the mouth of Teton River in the Sioux country. When the firm sold out to the American Fur Company in the fall of 1830, he entered the service of that company.

In later years Cerré was active in state and local politics, serving in the Missouri Legislature in 1848, as clerk of the St. Louis Circuit Court, and as sheriff of St. Louis County. He died January 5, 1860.

[38] Joseph Reddeford Walker, Bonneville's other assistant, was the son of a pioneer settler on Tennessee River, Joel P. Walker. He was born in a cabin in Roane County, a few miles west of Knoxville, December 13, 1798. He moved to Missouri in 1818, and two years later joined a party of trappers bound for Santa Fe by way of the Rockies. From 1827 to 1831 he served as the first sheriff of Jackson County, Missouri. In 1831, while on a journey southward to trade for horses, he met Captain Bonneville and agreed to go with him on his proposed trading expedition to the West as guide and lieutenant. Walker is best remembered as the commander of Bonneville's detached party which traveled to California and the Pacific and returned to Bonneville's Bear Lake rendezvous in 1833-34. He served as Bonneville's lieutenant in charge of trading and trapping operations in the Crow country during the fall, winter, and spring of 1834-35. Walker remained in the mountains until 1839. In 1845 he guided Frémont's third expedition across the Great Basin to California. He died in Contra Costa County, California, October 27, 1876.

Probably none of the mountain men, with the possible exception of Jedediah Smith, had a better knowledge of the geography of the west than did Joseph

of the Pacific, and for that purpose hired with Mr. Walker as clerk for a certain sum per year. The 20th of August was fixed as the day for each company to take its departure.[39] When the day arrived everything was in readiness—each man provided with four horses, and an equal share of blankets, buffalo robes, provisions, and every article necessary for the comfort of men engaged in an expedition of this kind. As we traveled along each man appeared in better spirits, and more lively than on any other similar occasion—and I sometimes thought that we were now on an expedition from which we would realize some profit. On the fourth day of our journey we arrived at the huts of some Bawnack Indians. These Indians appear to live very poor and in the most forlorn condition. They generally make but one visit to the buffalo country during the year, where they remain until they jirk as much meat as their females can lug home on their backs. They then quit the mountains and return to the plains, where they subsist on fish and small game the remainder of the year. They keep no horses, are always an easy prey for other Indians provided with guns and horses. On telling these Indians the route we intended to take, they told us we must provide ourselves with meat enough to subsist upon for many days—which we found to be very good advice. We now set to work laying in a stack of provision, and in a few days each man was provided with about sixty pounds of substantial meat, which was packed upon our horses, and we set sail in good cheer.

On the 4th of September we killed our last buffalo on the west side of the Salt Lake. We still continued along the margin of the Lake, with the intention of leaving it when we got to the extreme west side of it. About the 12th we found the country very poor, and almost without game, except goats and some few rab-

Reddeford Walker. Douglas S. Watson's *West Wind: The Life of Joseph Reddeford Walker* is an excellent biography of this remarkable man. And Daniel Ellis Conner's *Joseph Reddeford Walker and the Arizona Adventure* (Donald J. Berthrong and Odessa Davenport, (eds.) supplies an excellent portrait of this leader in action in 1862.

[39] The Walker party left the Green River rendezvous on July 24, 1833. Leonard's dating of this departure and of subsequent movements of the expedition is several weeks too late.

bits.[40] On the 13th we left the Lake and took a westerly course into the most extensive and barren plains I ever seen. This day we came to a spring, where we found some Indians encamped, who were on their way up to the buffalo country, to lay in their winter's supply of meat. These Indians appear to be more wealthy, and exercise more ingenuity in providing for themselves than those we had met with a few days ago. They have paths beat from one spring or hole of water to another, and by observing these paths, they told us, we would be enabled to find water without much trouble. The chief of this tribe further told us, that after traveling so many days southwest (the course we were now about to take), we would come to a high mountain which was covered with snow at the top the whole year round, and on each side of which we would find a large river to head and descend into the sandy plains below, forming innumerable small lakes, and sinks into the earth and disappears. Some distance further down these plains, he said, we would come to another mountain, much larger than the first, which he had never been across. In all this space, he said, there was no game; but that near this latter mountain we would come across a tribe of poor Indians, whom he supposed would not be friendly.

On the next morning we left these Indians and pursued our course northwest. Our men, who were in such fine spirits when we left the rendezvous, began to show symptoms of fatigue and were no longer so full of sport. We traveled along these paths according to the directions of the Indians, now and then meeting with a few straggling natives, who were in a manner naked, on the trail of the main body to the buffalo country. Some of these straggling Indians showed us some lumps of salt, which was the most white, clear and beautiful I ever seen.

On the 30th we arrived at a considerable hill, which, in appearance, is similar to a smooth rock, where we encamped for the night, and let our horses loose to graze—which we thought might now be done with safety, as we were no longer beset by

[40] The expedition had reached the barren Salt Lake desert in a little over three weeks' travel from the Green River rendezvous.

the murderous Rickarees. While laying about resting ourselves, some of the men observed the horses very eagerly licking the stones which lay on the surface of the ground near the spring. This circumstance caused the men to examine the stones, which we found to be salt, and had been carried here from the hill by the Indians. Their surface was covered with moss or rust, but on breaking them, or rubbing off the rust, the salt is seen in its purity. This hill runs north and south, and is from one to three miles across, and produces no kind of vegetation whatever except a little grass which grows in holes or gutters around its base, formed by water descending from the hill during the rainy season. This country appeared the most like a desert of any I had yet seen. It is so dry and sandy that there is scarcely any vegetation to be found—not even a spear of grass, except around the springs. The water in some of these springs, too, is so salt that it is impossible to drink it. The Indians say that it never rains, only in the spring of the year. Everything here seems to declare that, here man shall not dwell.*

After traveling a few days longer through these barren plains; we came to the mountain described by the Indian as having its peak covered with snow. It presents a most singular appearance —being entirely unconnected with any other chain. It is surrounded on either side by level plains, and rises abruptly to a great height, rugged and hard to ascend. To take a view of the surrounding country from this mountain, the eye meets with nothing but a smooth, sandy, level plain. On the whole, this mountain may be set down as one of the most remarkable phenomena of nature. Its top is covered with the pinone tree, bearing a kind of must, which the natives are very fond of, and which they collect for winter provision. This hill is nearly round, and looks like a hill or mound, such as may be met with in the prairies on the east side of the mountain.[41]

Not far from our encampment we found the source of the

---

* This hill was seen in 1824, by a Mr. Smith, who extended his explorations to the Pacific Coast, and was there taken prisoner by the Spaniards. See his travels.

[41] This mountain is present Pilot Peak.

river mentioned by the Indian. After we all got tired gazing at this mountain and the adjacent curiosities, we left it and followed down the river, in order to find water and grass for our horses. On this stream we found old signs of beaver, and we supposed that, as game was scarce in this country, the Indians had caught them for provision. The natives which we occasionally met with, still continued to be of the most poor and dejected kind—being entirely naked and very filthy. We came to the hut of one of these Indians who happened to have a considerable quantity of fur collected. At this hut we obtained a large robe composed of beaver skins fastened together, in exchange for two awls and one fish hook. This robe was worth from thirty to forty dollars. We continued traveling down this river, now and then catching a few beaver. But, as we continued to extend our acquaintance with the natives, they began to practice their national failing of stealing. So eager were they to possess themselves of our traps, that we were forced to quit trapping in this vicinity and make for some other quarter. The great annoyance we sustained in this respect greatly displeased some of our men, and they were for taking vengeance before we left the country—but this was not the disposition of Captain Walker. These discontents being out hunting one day, fell in with a few Indians, two or three of whom they killed, and then returned to camp, not daring to let the Captain know it. The next day while hunting, they repeated the same violation—but this time not quite so successful, for the Captain found it out, and immediately took measures for its effectual suppression.

At this place, all the branches of this stream is collected from the mountain into the main channel, which forms quite a large stream; and to which we gave the name of Barren River—a name which we thought would be quite appropriate, as the country, natives and everything belonging to it, justly deserves the name.[42] You may travel for many days on the banks of this river, without finding a stick large enough to make a walking cane. While we were on its margin, we were compelled to do without

[42] Leonard's Barren River is the Humboldt, which flows southwestward into the Humboldt Sink.

fire, unless we chanced to come across some drift that had collected together on the beach. As we proceeded down the river we found that the trails of the Indians began to look as if their numbers were increasing, ever since our men had killed some of their brethren. The further we descended the river, the more promising the country began to appear, although it still retained its dry, sandy nature. We had now arrived within view of a cluster of hills or mounds, which presented the appearance, from a distance, of a number of beautiful cities built up together. Here we had the pleasure of seeing timber, which grew in very sparing quantities some places along the river beach.

On the 4th of September we arrived at some lakes, formed by this river, which we supposed to be those mentioned by the Indian chief whom we met at the Great Salt Lake.[43] Here the country is low and swampy, producing an abundance of very fine grass—which was very acceptable to our horses, as it was the first good grazing they had been in for a long time—and here, on the borders of one of these lakes, we encamped, for the purpose of spending the night and letting our horses have their satisfaction. A little before sunset, on taking a view of the surrounding waste with a spy-glass, we discovered smoke issuing from the high grass in every direction. This was sufficient to convince us that we were in the midst of a large body of Indians; but as we could see no timber to go to, we concluded that it would be as well to remain in our present situation and defend ourselves as well as we could. We readily guessed that these Indians were in arms to revenge the death of those which our men had killed up the river; and if they could succeed in getting any advantage over us, we had no expectation that they would give us any quarter. Our first care, therefore, was to secure our horses, which we did by fastening them all together, and then hitching them to pickets drove into the ground. This done, we commenced constructing something for our own safety. The lake was immediately in our rear, and piling up all our baggage

---

[43] The expedition had arrived at Humboldt Lake in present Nevada. The date given by Leonard may not be far from the correct one.

69

in front, we had quite a substantial breastwork—which would have been as impregnable to the Indian's arrow as were the cotton bags to the British bullets at New Orleans in 1815. Before we had got everything completed, however, the Indians issued from their hiding places in the grass, to the number, as near as I could guess, of eight or nine hundred, and marched straight toward us, dancing and singing in the greatest glee. When within about 150 yards of us, they all sat down on the ground, and despatched five of their chiefs to our camp to inquire whether their people might come in and smoke with us. This request Captain Walker very prudently refused, as they evidently had no good intentions, but told them that he was willing to meet them half way between our breastwork, and where their people were then sitting. This appeared to displease them very much, and they went back not the least bit pleased with the reception they had met with.

After the five deputies related the result of their visit to their constituents, a part of them rose up and signed to us (which was the only mode of communicating with them) that they were coming to our camp. At this ten or twelve of our men mounted the breastwork and made signs to them that if they advanced a step further it was at the peril of their lives. They wanted to know in what way we would do it. Our guns were exhibited as the weapons of death. This they seemed to discredit and only laughed at us. They then wanted to see what effect our guns would have on some ducks that were then swimming in the lake, not far from the shore. We then fired at the ducks—thinking by this means to strike terror into the savages and drive them away. The ducks were killed, which astonished the Indians a good deal, though not so much as the noise of the guns—which caused them to fall flat to the ground. After this they put up a beaver skin on a bank for us to shoot at for their gratification—when they left us for the night. This night we stationed a strong guard, but no Indians made their appearance, and were permitted to pass the night in pleasant dreams.

Early in the morning we resumed our journey along the

lakes without seeing any signs of the Indians until after sunrise, when we discovered them issuing from the high grass in front, rear, and on either side of us. This created great alarm among our men, at first, as we thought they had surrounded us on purpose, but it appeared that we had only *happened* amongst them, and they were as much frightened as us. From this we turned our course from the border of the lake into the plain. We had not traveled far until the Indians began to move after us—first in small numbers, but presently in large companies. They did not approach near until we had traveled in this way for several hours, when they began to send small parties in advance, who would solicit us most earnestly to stop and smoke with them. After they had repeated this several times, we began to understand their motive—which was to detain us in order to let their whole force come up and surround us, or to get into close quarters with us, when their bows and arrows would be as fatal and more effective than our firearms. We now began to be a little stern with them, and gave them to understand that if they continued to trouble us they would do it at their own risk. In this manner we were teased until a party of eighty or one hundred came forward, who appeared more saucy and bold than any others. This greatly excited Captain Walker, who was naturally of a very cool temperament, and he gave orders for the charge, saying that there was nothing equal to a good start in such a case. This was sufficient. A number of our men had never been engaged in any fighting with the Indians, and were anxious to try their skill. When our commander gave his consent to chastise these Indians, and give them an idea of our strength, 32 of us dismounted and prepared ourselves to give a severe blow. We tied our extra horses to some shrubs and left them with the main body of our company, and then selected each a choice steed, mounted and surrounded this party of Indians. We closed in on them and fired, leaving thirty-nine dead on the field—which was nearly the half—the remainder were overwhelmed with dismay—running into the high grass in every direction, howling in the most lamentable manner.

Captain Walker then gave orders to some of the men to take the bows of the fallen Indians and put the wounded out of misery. The severity with which we dealt with these Indians may be revolting to the heart of the philanthropist; but the circumstances of the case altogether atones for the cruelty. It must be borne in mind that we were far removed from the hope of any succor in case we were surrounded, and that the country we were in was swarming with hostile savages, sufficiently numerous to devour us. Our object was to strike a decisive blow. This we did—even to a greater extent than we had intended.[44]

These Indians are totally naked—both male and female—with the exception of a shield of grass, which they wear around their loins. They are generally small and weak, and some of them very hairy. They subsist upon grass-seed, frogs, fish, &c.—Fish, however, are very scarce—their manner of catching which is somewhat novel and singular. They take the leg-bone of a sand-hill crane, which is generally about eighteen inches long, this is fastened in the end of a pole—they then, by means of a raft made of rushes, which are very plenty—float along the surface of these lakes and spear the fish. They exhibit great dexterity with this simple structure—sometimes killing a fish with it at a great distance. They also have a kind of hook by which they sometimes are very successful, but it does not afford them as much sport as the spear. This hook is formed of a small bone, ground down on a sand-stone, and a double beard cut in it with a flint—they then have a line made of wild flax. This line is tied nearest the beard end of the hook, by pulling the line the sharp end with the beard, catches, and turns the bone crossways in its mouth.

[44] Irving harshly criticized the expedition for wantonly killing "poor savages" who "had no hostile intention." *Adventures of Captain Bonneville*, 387–89. However, the actions of the trappers were not unprovoked. The Indians had stolen valuable beaver traps from them. Walker did not condone those initial killings. But when large numbers of Indians, armed with bows and arrows (which were not ineffective weapons in the hands of skilled bowmen), dogged the party's footsteps, even mild-mannered Walker grew suspicious of their intentions. His actions were swift and decisive. The Indians, probably Paiutes, no longer bothered the exploring party.

These lakes are all joined together by means of the river which passes from one to another, until it reaches the largest, which has no outlet. The water in this lake becomes stagnant and very disagreeable—its surface being covered with a green substance, similar to a stagnant frog pond. In warm weather there is a fly, about the size and similar to a grain of wheat, on this lake, in great numbers. When the wind rolls the waters onto the shore, these flies are left on the beach—the female Indians then carefully gather them into baskets made of willow branches, and lay them exposed to the sun until they become perfectly dry, when they are laid away for winter provender. These flies, together with grass seed, and a few rabbits, is their principal food during the winter season.

Their habitations are formed of a round hole dug in the ground, over which sticks are placed, giving it the shape of a potato hole—this is covered with grass and earth—the door at one side and the fire at the other. They cook in a pot made of stiff mud, which they lay upon the fire and burn; but from the sandy nature of the mud, after cooking a few times, it falls to pieces, when they make a new one.

These Indians call themselves Shoshocoes;[45] and the Lakes have been named Battle Lakes.

On the 10th of October we left these Indians and built rafts out of rushes to convey us across the river, when we left the lakes and continued our course in the direction of a large mountain, which was in sight, and which we could see was covered with snow on the summit. In the evening we encamped on the margin of a large lake formed by a river which heads in this mountain. This lake, likewise, has no outlet for the water, except that which sinks into the ground. The water in this lake is similar to lie, and tastes much like pearlash. If this river was in the vicinity of some city, it would be of inestimable value, as it is admirably calculated to wash clothes without soap, and no doubt

[45] Shoshocoes ("Walkers") was not a tribal name. It was a general term applied to the poorer bands and to individuals among the Shoshonean tribes who owned no horses. Frederick Webb Hodge, *Handbook of American Indians North of Mexico*, I, 554.

73

could be appropriated to many valuable uses. There is also a great quantity of pumice stone floating on the surface of the water, and the shore is covered with them. The next day we traveled up this river towards the mountain, where we encamped for the night.[46] This mountain is very high, as the snow extends down the side nearly half way—the mountain runs north and south.

In the morning we despatched hunters to the mountain in search of game and also to look out for a pass over the mountain, as our provisions were getting scarce—our dried buffalo meat being almost done. After prowling about all day, our hunters returned in the evening, bringing the unwelcome tidings that they had not seen any signs of game in all their ramblings, and what was equally discouraging, that they had seen no practicable place for crossing the mountain. They, however, had with them a young colt and camel, which they secured by the natives taking fright and running off, when the hunters came in sight.[47] The next morning, having eaten the last of our dried buffalo meat, it was decided that the colt should be killed and divided equally to each man. Our situation was growing worse every hour, and something required to be done to extricate ourselves. Our horses were reduced very much from the fatigues of our journey and light food, having traveled through a poor, sandy country extending from the buffalo country of the Rocky Mountains to our present encampment, a distance of about twelve hundred miles, without encountering a single hill of any consequence (with the exception of the one in which Barren River heads, and that we went around) and so poor and bare that nothing can subsist on it with the exception of rabbits—these being the only game we had met with since we had left the buffalo country, with the exception of one or two antelopes. Notwithstanding these plains forbid the support of animals of every description, yet I do not

[46] Douglas Watson was of the opinion that the party moved up Walker River to the vicinity of present Bridgeport, Mono County, California. *West Wind*, 56.

[47] Undoubtedly Leonard's editor misread Leonard's manuscript here. Leonard may have written "mule" rather than "camel." Certainly there were no camels in this region in 1833.

believe that we passed a single day without seeing Indians, or fresh signs, and some days hundreds of them. Today we sent out several scouting parties to search out a pass over the mountain. Captain Walker, Nidever and myself started out together. After getting part of the way up the mountain we came to a grove of timber, where the mountain was too steep for our horses, and we left them, and traveled on foot. Nidever was separated from us, when two Indians made their appearance, but as soon as they saw us, they took to flight and run directly towards Nidever, who at once supposed they had been committing some mischief with us, fired, and, as they were running one behind the other, killed them both at one shot. After this unpleasant circumstance we went back to our horses, and from thence to camp. Mr. Nidever was very sorry when he discovered what he had done.[48] In the evening the balance of our scouting parties returned, but none of them had killed any game. One of them had found an Indian path, which they thought led over the mountain—whereupon it was resolved that in the morning we would take this path, as it seemed to be our only prospect of preservation. Accordingly, at an early hour the next morning we started on our journey along the foot of the mountain in search of the path discovered on the previous day, and found it. On examination we found that horses traveled it, and must of course come from the west. This gave us great encouragement, as we were very fearful we would not be able to get our horses over at all. Here we encamped for the night. In the morning we started on our toilsome journey. Ascending the mountain we found to be very difficult from the rocks and its steepness. This day we made but poor speed, and encamped on the side of the mountain.

October 16. Continued our course until in the afternoon, when we arrived at what we took for the top, where we again encamped, but without anything to eat for our horses, as the

[48] This was George Nidever, a veteran of the Battle of Pierre's Hole and a member of the Walker party, who has left a brief account of the expedition. William Henry Ellison (ed.), *The Life and Adventures of George Nidever, 1802–1883*, 32–34.

ground was covered with a deep snow, which from appearance, lays on the north side of the peaks the whole year around.[49] These peaks are generally covered with rocks and sand, totally incapable of vegetation; except on the south side, where grows a kind of juniper or gin shrub, bearing a berry tasting similar to gin. Here we passed the night without anything to eat except these gin berries, and some of the insects from the lake described above, which our men had got from the Indians. We had not suffered much from cold for several months previous to this; but this night, surrounded as we were with the everlasting snows on the summit of this mountain, the cold was felt with three-fold severity.

In taking a view the next morning of the extensive plains through which we had traveled, its appearance is awfully sublime. As far as the eye can reach, you can see nothing but an unbroken level, tiresome to the eye to behold. To the east the aspect is truly wonderful. The sight meets with nothing but a poor sandy plain, extending from the base of the Rocky Mountains to the level below—interposed with several rivers winding their way, here and there forming innumerable lakes, having their margins thinly adorned with a few withering and fading cottonwood trees—where the water ceases to flow, and sinks into the sand. But this is not all. The rivers which head in this mountain all lead towards the east, as if to meet those from the Rocky Mountains, and likewise empty into the lakes. The next morning it was with no cheerful prospect that each man prepared himself for traveling, as we had nothing to eat worth mentioning. As we advanced, in the hollows sometimes we would encounter prodigious quantities of snow. When we would come to such places, a certain portion of the men would be appointed alternately to go forward and break the road, to enable our horses to get through; and if any of the horses would get swamped, these same men were to get them out. In this tedious and tire-

[49] The exact course followed by the Walker party in this first recorded westbound crossing of the Sierras is not known. Probably they ascended by one of the southern tributaries of the East Walker River.

Indians of the Great Basin

From a Field Sketch by H. V. A. von Bekh, 1859

The Sierra Nevada from Carson Lake

From a Field Sketch by H. V. A. von Bekh, 1859

some manner we spent the whole day without going more than eight or ten miles. In some of these ravines where the snow is drifted from the peaks, it never entirely melts, and may be found at this season of the year from ten to one hundred feet deep. From appearance it never melts on the top, but in warm weather the heap sinks by that part melting which lays next the ground. This day's travel was very severe on our horses, as they had not a particle to eat. They began to grow stupid and stiff, and we began to despair of getting them over the mountain. We encamped this night on the south side of one of these peaks or ridges without anything to eat, and almost without fire. To add to the troubles and fatigues which we encountered in the day time, in getting over the rocks and through the snow, we had the mortification this evening to find that some of our men had become almost unmanageable, and were desirous of turning back and retracing our steps to the buffalo country! The voice of the majority, which always directs the movements of such a company, would not pacify them; nor had the earnest appeals of our captain any effect. The distance was too great for them to undertake without being well provided, and the only way they could be prevented, was by not letting them have any of the horses or ammunition. Two of our horses were so much reduced that it was thought they would not be able to travel in the morning at all, whereupon it was agreed that they should be butchered for the use of the men. This gave our men fresh courage, and we went to bed this night in better spirits than we had done for a long time. Some of the men had fasted so long, and were so much in want of nourishment, that they did not know when they had satisfied the demands of nature, and eat as much and as eagerly of this black, tough, lean, horse flesh, as if it had been the choicest piece of beef steak.

In the morning, after freely partaking of the horse meat, and sharing the remainder to each man, we renewed our journey, now and then coming onto an Indian path, but as they did not lead in the direction we were going, we did not follow them— but the most of the distance we this day traveled, we had to encounter hills, rocks and deep snows. The snow in most of the hollows we this day passed through, looks as if it had remained here all summer, as eight or ten inches from the top it was packed close and firm—the top being loose and light, having fell only a day or two previous. About the middle of the afternoon we arrived at a small lake or pond, where we concluded to encamp, as at this pond we found a small quantity of very indifferent grass, but which our horses cropped off with great eagerness. Here we spent the night, having yet seen nothing to create a hope that we had arrived near the opposite side of the mountain—and what was equally as melancholy, having yet discovered no signs of game.

The next morning we resumed our labor, fortunately finding less snow and more timber, besides a number of small lakes, and some prospect of getting into a country that produced some kind of vegetation. The timber is principally pine, cedar, and red wood, mostly of a scrubby and knotty quality. After traveling a few miles further, however, than any other day since we had reached the top of the mountain, we again encamped on the margin of another small lake, where we also had the good fortune to find some pasture for our horses. This evening it was again decided to kill three more of our horses which had grown entirely worthless from severe traveling and little food. The next morning several parties were despatched on search of a pass over the mountain, and to make search for game; but they all returned in the evening without finding either. The prospect at this time began to grow somewhat gloomy and threaten us with hard times again. We were at a complete stand. No one was acquainted with the country, nor no person knew how wide the summit of this mountain was. We had traveled for five days since we arrived at what we supposed to be the summit—were now still surrounded with snow and rugged peaks—the vigor of every man almost exhausted—nothing to give our poor horses, which were no longer any assistance to us in traveling, but a burthen, for we had to help the most of them along as we would an old and feeble man.

This mountain must be near as high as the main chain of the Rocky Mountains—at least a person would judge so from the vast quantity of snow with which it is covered, and the coldness of the air. The descent from the Rocky Mountains to this is but trifling, and supposed by all the company not to be greater than we had ascended this mountain from the plain—though we had no means of ascertaining the fact. It is true, however, that the vast plain through which we had traveled was almost perfectly level, on part of which the water gradually descended to the west, and on the other towards the east.

Our situation was growing more distressing every hour, and all we now thought of was to extricate ourselves from this inhospitable region; and, as we were perfectly aware, that to travel on foot was the only way of succeeding, we spent no time in idleness—scarcely stopping in our journey to view an occasional specimen of the wonders of nature's handiwork. We traveled a few miles every day, still on the top of the mountain, and our course continually obstructed with snow, hills and rocks. Here we began to encounter in our path, many small streams which would shoot out from under these high snowbanks, and after running a short distance in deep chasms which they have through ages cut in the rocks, precipitate themselves from one lofty precipice to another, until they are exhausted in rain below. Some of these precipices appeared to us to be more than a mile high. Some of the men thought that if we could succeed in descending one of these precipices to the bottom, we might thus work our way into the valley below—but on making several attempts we found it utterly impossible for a man to descend, to say nothing of our horses. We were then obliged to keep along the top of the dividing ridge between two of these chasms which seemed to lead pretty near in the direction we were going—which was west—in passing over the mountain, supposing it to run north and south.[50] In this manner we continued until the 25th

---

[50] The party moved westward along the divide between the Merced and Tuolumne rivers within the area of the present Yosemite National Park. From these heights it is probable that members of the expedition were the first white

without any particular occurrence, except that of our horses dying daily—the flesh of which we preserved for food. Our course was very rough and tiresome, having to encounter one hill of snow and one ledge of rocks after another. On the 25th every man appeared to be more discouraged and down-spirited than ever, and I thought that our situation would soon be beyond hope if no prospect of getting from the mountain would now be discovered. This day we sent out several parties on discoveries, who returned in the evening without bringing the least good news, except one man, who was last coming, having separated from his companions, brought a basket full of acorns to camp. These were the first acorns we had seen since we left the state of Missouri. These nuts our hunter had got from an Indian who had them on his back traveling as though he was on a journey across the mountain, to the east side. When the Indian seen our hunter he dropped his basket of provision and run for life.[51] These nuts caused no little rejoicing in our camp, not only on account of their value as food, but because they gave us the gratifying evidence that a country mild and salubrious enough to produce acorns was not far distant, which must be vastly different from any we had passed through for a long time. We now felt agreeably surprised that we had succeeded so far and so prosperously, in a region of many miles in extent where a native Indian could find nothing to eat in traversing the same route, but acorns. These nuts are quite different from those in Missouri—being much larger and more palatable. They are from one and one-half to three inches in length, and about three-fourths in diameter, and when roasted in the ashes or broiled, are superior to any chesnuts I ever eat—(though a person subsisting upon very lean horse meat for several days is hardly capable of judging with precision in a case of this kind).

---

men to view the magnificent Yosemite Valley. Carl P. Russell, the historian of Yosemite National Park, recognizes the Walker party as "the discoverer" of the Yosemite Valley. *One Hundred Years in Yosemite*, 6–7.

[51] This may have been one of the Yosemite (Grizzly Bear) Indians, a subdivision of the Miwok inhabiting the Yosemite Valley before it was given that name in 1851.

The next morning we resumed our journey somewhat revived with the strong expectation that after a few days more tedious traveling, we would find ourselves in a country producing some kind of game by which we might recruit our languid frames, and pasture to resuscitate the famished condition of our horses. We still found snow in abundance, but our course was not so much obstructed with rocks as formerly. In two or three days we arrived at the brink of the mountain. This at first was a happy sight, but when we approached close, it seemed to be so near perpendicular that it would be folly to attempt a descent. In looking on the plain below with the naked eye, you have one of the most singular prospects in nature; from the great height of the mountain the plain presents a dim yellow appearance; but on taking a view with the spy glass we found it to be a beautiful plain stretched out towards the west until the horizon presents a barrier to the sight. From the spot where we stood to the plain beneath, must at least be a distance of three miles, as it is almost perpendicular, a person cannot look down without feeling as if he was wafted to and fro in the air, from the giddy height. A great many were the surmises as to the distance and direction to the nearest point of the Pacific. Captain Walker, who was a man well acquainted with geography, was of the opinion that it was not much further than we could see with the aid of our glass, as the plain had the appearance of a sea shore. Here we encamped for the night, and sent men out to discover some convenient passage down towards the plain—who returned after an absence of a few hours and reported that they had discovered a pass or Indian trail which they thought would answer our purpose, and also some signs of deer and bear, which was equally as joyful news— as we longed to have a taste of some palatable food. The next morning after pursuing our course a few miles along the edge of the mountain top we arrived at the path discovered by our men, and immediately commenced the descent, gladly leaving the cold and famished region of snow behind. The mountain was extremely steep and difficult to descend, and the only way we could come any speed was by taking a zigzag direction, first

81

climbing along one side and then turning to the other, until we arrived at a ledge or precipice of rocks, of great height, and extending eight or ten miles along the mountain—where we halted and sent men in each direction to ascertain if there was any possibility of getting over this obstruction. In the afternoon of the same day our men returned without finding any safe passage through the rocks—but one man had succeeded in killing a small deer, which he carried all the way to camp on his back—this was dressed, cooked and eat in less time than a hungry wolf would devour a lamb.

This was the first game larger than a rabbit we had killed since the 4th of August when we killed the last buffalo near the Great Salt Lake, and the first we had eat since our dried meat was exhausted (being fourteen days), during which time we lived on stale and forbidden horse flesh. I was conscious that it was not such meat as a dog would feast on, but we were driven to extremes and had either to do this or die. It was the most unwholesome as well as the most unpleasant food I ever eat or ever expect to eat—and I hope that no other person will ever be compelled to go through the same. It seemed to be the greatest cruelty to take your rifle, when your horse sinks to the ground from starvation, but still manifests a desire and willingness to follow you, to shoot him in the head and then cut him up and take such parts of their flesh as extreme hunger alone will render it possible for a human being to eat. This we done several times, and it was the only thing that saved us from death. Twenty-four of our horses died since we arrived on top of the mountain—seventeen of which we eat the best parts.

When our men returned without finding any passage over the rocks, we searched for a place that was as smooth and gradual in the descent as possible, and after finding one we brought our horses, and by fastening ropes round them let them down one at a time without doing them any injury. After we got our horses and baggage all over the rocks we continued our course down the mountain, which still continued very steep and difficult. The circumstance of one of our men killing a deer greatly cheered the languid spirits of our hunters, and after we got safely over the rocks several of the men started out in search of game, although it was then near night. The main body continued on down until we arrived at some green oak bushes, where we encamped for the night, to wait for our hunters—who returned soon after dark well paid for their labor, having killed two large black tailed deer and a black bear, and all very fat and in good eating order. This night we passed more cheerful and in better heart than any we had spent for a long time. Our meat was dressed and well cooked, and every man felt in good order to partake of it.

In descending the mountain this far we have found but little snow, and began to emerge into a country which had some signs of vegetation—having passed through several groves of green oak bushes, &c. The principal timber which we came across is red wood, white cedar, and the balsam tree. We continued down the side of the mountain at our leisure, finding the timber much larger and better, game more abundant and the soil more fertile. Here we found plenty of oak timber, bearing a large quantity of acorns, though of a different kind from those taken from the Indian on the mountain top. In the evening of the 30th we arrived at the foot or base of this mountain—having spent almost a month in crossing over. Along the base of this mountain it is quite romantic—the soil is very productive—the timber is immensely large and plenty, and game, such as deer, elk, grizzly bear and antelopes are remarkably plenty. From the mountain out to the plain, a distance varying from ten to twenty miles, the timber stands as thick as it could grow, and the land is well watered by a number of small streams rising here and there along the mountain. In the last two days traveling we have found some trees of the red-wood species, incredibly large— some of which would measure from sixteen to eighteen fathom round the trunk and at the height of a man's head from the ground.[52]

[52] Leonard's entry is the first published reference to the Big Trees of California. Russell, on the basis of Leonard's statement, credits the Walker party

On the 31st we pursued our course towards the plain in a western direction. Now that we had reached a country thickly filled with almost all kinds of game, our men, and particularly those fond of hunting, were in fine spirits. This day our company was much scattered, and we could hardly tell which was the main body, as the men were stretched over a large space of ground, all moving within each other's hearing towards the plain. After a walk of about fifteen miles we arrived at the margin of the woods, where we concluded to spend the remainder of the day and night. When our men all gathered together it was astonishing to see the quantity of game which they had collected—principally deer and bear. Our hunters complained very much because there was no buffalo here—as killing these animals afford the hunter such fine sport; and they would not believe anything else than that buffalo inhabited this region until they had made several unsuccessful hunts—as the climate and soil is about the same, the grass equally as good and plenty, and the prairies and forests as extensive as those of the region of the Rocky Mountains. But none of these animals have ever been found west of the Great Salt Lake, which is about three hundred miles west of the summit of the Rocky Mountains.[53]

On the following morning we directed our course across or rather along the plain, until we came to a large river heading in the mountain and wending its way through the plain. This river presents more wonderful curiosities than any other stream we passed. Its bed lays very deep forming very high banks, even in smooth and level parts of the country; but where there is rocks

---

with the discovery of the giant redwood trees, *Sequoia gigantea.* Whether they saw the Merced Grove or the Tuolumne Grove cannot be definitely determined. *One Hundred Years in Yosemite,* 8.

[53] C. Hart Merriam, "The Buffalo in Northeastern California," *Journal of Mammalogy,* Vol. 7, No. 3 (1926), 211–14, concluded that the buffalo did not push westward beyond the *south* end of Great Salt Lake, that there is no record of its occurrence on the west side of Salt Lake, or in the valley of Humboldt River, or anywhere in the vast desert region between Great Salt Lake and California. However, the buffalo did enter California and a narrow strip along the extreme western border of northern Nevada from the *north.*

its appearance is beyond doubt the most remarkable of any other water course. Some places the rocks are piled up perpendicular to such a height that a man on top, viewed from the bed of the river, does not look larger than a small child. From the appearance of these precipices it is not exaggerating to state that they may be found from a quarter to half a mile high—and many of them no wider at the top than at the bottom. Through such places the river forces its way with great rapidity, tossing, pitching and foaming to such a degree that no Indian has the courage to attempt to navigate it with his canoe. When the water passes through these *narrows* it spreads out in a beautiful deep bay as if to repose after its turbulent dashing against the rocks immediately above, until it reaches the next rapids, when it again pitches forward. This plain is well watered and is quite productive, as we found a large quantity of wild pumpkins and wild oats.[54]

This night it was decided that we should forthwith commence trapping for furs and make this expedition as profitable as possible, for, as yet we had spent much time and toil, and lost many horses, without realizing any profit whatever—although every man expressed himself fully compensated for his labor, by the many natural curiosities which we had discovered. According to the arrangements made on the evening previous, we all the next morning commenced traveling down the river at a slow gate, carefully examining for beaver signs, and recruiting our horses, which they had much need of, as we found them to be much more injured in crossing the mountains than we had at first supposed—many of them being sprained and stiffened almost beyond recovery, and certainly beyond present use. We laid up a large supply of deer, elk, and bear meat, of the best kind. These animals are the fattest of the kind I had ever eat. Here we found a large quantity of acorns, such as those taken from the Indian. These acorns compose the principal food of the

[54] The party apparently was proceeding down the valley of the Merced River to the broad valley of the San Joaquín.

wild animals in this section—the bear, I believe, solely subsists upon them, and where acorns are scarce, the game is both poor and scarce.

The country here appears to be in many respects similar to the east side of the Rocky Mountains. The land is generally smooth and level, and the plains or prairies are very extensive, stretching towards the setting sun as far as the eye can reach; whilst a number of beautiful rivers, all heading in this rugged mountain, running parallel with each other through the plain, also to the west, with their banks handsomely adorned with flourishing timber of different kinds, such as blackwalnut, hickory, oak, elm, mulberry, hackberry, alder, sumac, &c. This grove of timber may be found along the river at any point, and generally extends about four miles into the plain. Between this grove of timber and the forest extending from the foot of the mountain, there is a level prairie of the richest soil, producing grass in abundance of the most delightful and valuable quality.

These prairies are in many places swarming with wild horses, some of which are quite docile, particularly the males, on seeing our horses. They are all very fat, and can be seen of all colors, from spotted or white, to jet blacks; and here, as in the land of civilization, they are the most beautiful and noble, as well as the most valuable of the whole brute creation.

Since we left the mountain we have seen many signs of Indians, such as moccasin tracks, and smoke rising from the prairies in different places, but as yet we had not succeeded in getting in company with any. At this season of the year, when the grass in these plains is dry, if a fire should be started it presents a spectacle truly grand—and if the flame is assisted with a favorable wind, it will advance with such speed that the wild horses and other animals are sometimes puzzled to get out of the road, and everything looks overwhelmed with consternation. We continued traveling down the river until the 7th of November, when we arrived at five Indian huts, containing fifteen or twenty Indians male and female. When they first beheld the approach of beings so mysterious as we were to them, they exhibited the most unbounded alarm and fear. But it was not long till we succeeded in calming their terror, and convincing them that they had no reason to apprehend any danger, by showing a willingness to smoke (this being the first token of friendship with all Indians), which they at once understood and immediately became reconciled, and we commenced gathering all the information from them that our limited means would afford—each being entirely ignorant of the other's language, and the Indians being extremely awkward both in making and understanding signs—which is the principal method of conversation with the different tribes in this region.[55] After making many efforts to get some information from them with reference to the Big Water, white people, beaver, &c., without receiving any further satisfaction by way of answer to our inquiries than a grunt similar to that of a hog, we concluded to spend the night with them for further trial. Towards night whilst passing through their camp, some of our men found two blankets and a knife, which convinced us at once that they had some communication with white people. When the blankets were held up to them they pronounced in tolerable distinctness, the word *Spanish*, and pointed to the west—from which circumstance we inferred that the Spanish settlement could not be far distant.

The next morning our Indian hosts brought some horses to the camp for the purpose of trading, which were marked with a Spanish brand. After trading for five of the best of their horses, for which we gave one yard of scarlet cloth and two knives; we left these Indians and continued down the river in search of beaver, which are very scarce. These Indians are quite small, and much darker than those of the buffalo country, as well as more indolent and slothful. They generally run naked with the exception of a few, who wear shields made of some kind of skins. Their huts are composed of dry polls or logs set upon end, and their bedding consists of grass. Their food is composed principally of horsemeat and acorns—the latter are very large and of good qual-

[55] The sign language, commonly employed by the Plains Indians in intertribal communications, was not known to the tribes of California.

87

ity, which they manufacture into a kind of mush. Their method of manufacturing this is as follows:—They go to a large log and build a fire upon it and burn it half or two-thirds of the way through, which is done by keeping the log wet except about a foot in diameter, where the fire is kept up until the hole is deep enough, and of the proper shape. After the hole is burnt deep enough they extinguish the fire, scrape out the coals and ashes, and have a tolerably well shaped *hopper.* When this is done they get a long stone which is rounded at one end, and put the acorns in and commence mashing them fine, which is easily done as they are always previously dried by fire or the sun. The meal thus made is then taken out and mixed with water in a basket made almost water-tight—which they broil by making stones red hot and throwing them into the basket. By this process they made a kind of mush with which any hungry man would be glad to satiate his appetite.

These Indians also appear very delicate and feeble—which they attribute to eating acorns. Today, whilst some of our hunters were searching for beaver signs along the river beach, they found the carcases of four Indians, two of which were partly consumed by grizzly bears. They appeared as if they had died natural deaths, and been laid there by their friends according to their custom of disposing of the dead, as two of them were well wrapped up in beaver skins. This day our course lay through a large prairie covered with wild oats—which at this season of the year when nothing but the stock remains, has much the appearance of common oats. This plain lays on the south side of the river, to which we gave the name of Oat Plain. The grizzly bear and wild horses appeared more numerous in the country through which we this day passed than I had ever before known them. In the evening just before sunset we came across the carcase of another Indian, which was also partly eaten by the wild beasts. From the numerous signs we were led to the belief that the country through which we were now traveling was thickly inhabited with Indians, but notwithstanding we kept watch both night and day we were unable to discover any but those we had left in the morning; nor could we find any of their habitations, although we would sometimes come across a trail that looked as if it was traversed by hundreds at a time.[56] We also discovered some signs of white people, as we would occasionally come across a tree or log chopped with an axe as if done by trappers and hunters. At this place the river is from two to three hundred yards wide, as the country is generally level the water moves gently forward, being quite deep, clear and smooth.[57] This night we encamped on the bank of the river in a very beautiful situation. Soon after the men went to rest and the camp had became quieted, we were startled by a loud distant noise similar to that of thunder. Whilst lying close to the ground this noise could be distinctly heard for a considerable length of time without intermission. When it was at first observed some of our men were much alarmed, as they readily supposed it was occasioned by an earthquake, and they began to fear that we would all be swallowed up in the bowels of the earth; and others judged it to be the noise of a neighboring cataract. Captain Walker, however, suggested a more plausible cause, which allayed the fears of the most timid. He supposed that the noise originated by the Pacific rolling and dashing her boisterous waves against the rocky shore. Had any of us ever before been at the coast, we would have readily accounted for the mysterious noise.

The idea of being within hearing of the *end* of the *Far West* inspired the heart of every member of our company with a patriotic feeling for his country's honor, and all were eager to lose no time until they should behold what they had heard. We felt as if all our previous hardships and privations would be adequately compensated, if we would be spared to return in safety to the homes of our kindred and have it to say that we had stood upon the extreme end of the great west. The two next

[56] Although the Indians of the San Joaquín Valley were Yokuts and those of the high country from which the party had descended were Miwok, both spoke dialects of the Penutian language.

[57] The party was now following the San Joaquín River northward toward its mouth.

days we traveled very fast without meeting with anything to impede our progress. On the night of the 12th our men were again thrown into great consternation by the singular appearance of the heavens. Soon after dark the air appeared to be completely thickened with meteors falling towards the earth, some of which would explode in the air and others would be dashed to pieces on the ground, frightening our horses so much that it required the most active vigilance of the whole company to keep them together. This was altogether a mystery to some of the men who probably had never before seen or heard of anything of the kind, but after an explanation from Captain Walker, they were satisfied that no danger need be apprehended from the falling of the stars, as they were termed.[58]

After traveling a few miles the next morning we arrived at the head of tide water, which convinced us that the noise we had heard a few days previous was created by the ocean. We continued down the river until we arrived at the bay, where it mingles its water with the briny ocean.[59] The country here lays very low, and looks as if it was subject to being overflowed. Here we found difficult traveling owing to the ground being wet and swampy. In the vicinity of this bay we found a great many Indians, who were mostly occupied in fishing—which are very plenty. These Indians appeared friendly enough, but then they manifested a kind of careless indifference, whether they treated us well or ill, that we did not like, and we therefore concluded to leave this place and make for the main coast as soon as possible—and accordingly we started in a southern direction and after traveling a day and a half the broad Pacific burst forth to view on the 20th.[60] The first night we encamped quite close

[58] This meteoric shower of November 12, 1833, was observed throughout the United States. Even though the date may have been supplied by Leonard's editor, mention of the phenomenon provides a check on the location of the Walker party at that time. They were nearing the mouth of the San Joaquín River.

[59] Douglas S. Watson (West Wind, 59) was of the opinion that the Walker party reached Suisan Bay in the vicinity of present-day Martinez.

[60] The Walker party had skirted the eastern shores of San Pablo and San Francisco bays, and had then crossed the Coast Range to the Pacific Ocean. Watson (West Wind, 59), was of the opinion that they reached the ocean in the vicinity of Ano Nuevo Point.

to the beach near a spring of delightful water. The scenes which we could now contemplate were quite different from those we had beheld and dwelt amidst for months back. Here was a smooth unbroken sheet of water stretched out far beyond the reach of the eye—altogether different from mountains, rocks, snows, and the toilsome plains we had traversed. Here we occasionally found the traces of white men, and as the Indians still appeared to act so strange, we began to think that the Spaniards had the Indians under complete subjection, and that they could, if so disposed, set them on us and give us trouble. It was therefore thought best to find out the whereabouts of the Spaniards and cultivate their friendship. The Indians here practice fishing to a great extent; indeed it seems to be the only thing they do. They have many methods of catching them—but the principal process is by spearing them with bones made sharp, and some have proper instruments of Spanish manufacture, in which they are very expert. The principal fish in the river we came down, and which has the principal Indian fisheries, are shad and salmon. We did not find out the name of this tribe, or whether they consider themselves distinct from any other tribe.[61] Most all of the natives we met with since crossing the last mountain, seem to belong to the same nation, as they were about the same color and size—spoke the same language for anything we could discover to the contrary, and all appeared equally ignorant and dilatory—and most of them entirely naked. They have no particular place of residence but claim the whole of the country stretching from the mountain to the seashore as their own. In some parts the natives raise a small quantity of corn, pumpkins, melons, &c., the soil being so very strong and mellow that it requires but little labor to raise good crops.

21st. This morning the ocean was not so calm as it was the previous evening. All its sleeping energies were lashed into fury, and the mountain waves of the great deep would roll and dash

---

[61] These Indian fishermen were Costanoans (Spanish: *Costaños*, "Coastmen"). They had been under the influence of Franciscan missionaries for more than half a century.

against the shore, producing the most deafening sound. In the course of the day a detachment of our company was despatched to make discoveries, who returned in the evening and stated that they had discovered many signs of white people, whom they supposed to be Spaniards, but they were unable to come up with them. This same party also found the carcass of a whale which was ninety feet long—the tusks weighing four and one-half pounds. About noon of the third day after we arrived here, the attention of the company was directed to an object which could be dimly seen at a distance riding on the water, which was immediately judged to be a ship, but no one knew from whence it came, where it belonged or where going. It was now our curiosity to know more of this singular object and if possible to attract their attention and bring them to shore. Accordingly we fastened two white blankets together and hoisted them into the air on a pole. This had the desired effect. It was not long until we could tell that the distance between us was fast diminishing, and our joy and surprise may be imagined when we beheld the broad stripes and bright stars of the American flag waving majestically in the air at the masthead. The ship anchored some distance from the shore and the boats were despatched to see what nation we belonged to, and what our business was. Their astonishment was equally as great as ours when they ascertained that we were children of the same nation of themselves. On making this discovery, and a signal to that effect being given by the boats, the ship fired several salutes of canon in honor of our meeting, which made the welkin ring. On further acquaintance we ascertained this ship (the *Lagoda*) to belong to Boston, commanded by Captain Baggshaw.[62] After exchanging civilities by shaking hands all round, Captain Baggshaw strongly insisted on us going on board and partaking of the ship's fare, stating that he had a few casks of untapped Coneac. This was an invitation that none of us had the least desire to refuse, and

[62] The master of the *Lagoda* was John Bradshaw. This ship of 292 tons was owned by Bryant and Sturgis of Boston, and was on the West Coast from the autumn of 1833 to the spring of 1835.

accordingly forty-five of us went on board the *Lagoda,* leaving the remainder to take care of the camp, &c. When arriving on the ship Captain B., had a table spread with the choicest of liquors and best fare the ship would afford, which was immediately surrounded with hungry captains, mates, clerks, sailors, and greasy trappers—after eating, the glass was passed around in quick succession, first drinking after the fashion of brave Jack Tars, and afterwards in the mountain style, mixed with something of the manners of the natives, in order to amuse the sailors.

After we got on board, the sea became very rough, causing the vessel to pitch and plunge a great deal as she lay at anchor, and consequently I was compelled to return to shore from sea sickness. The balance remained and kept up the celebration until daylight the next morning, when they all returned to land, accompanied by the ship's crew to taper off on the harder fare of the trapper and hunter. The feast on the vessel was far superior to anything we could give them, although they appeared perfectly satisfied with the reception they met with from us, as it was a long time since they had tasted any fresh meat, or anything but salted victuals; and theirs was the first bread, butter, cheese, &c., that we had seen for more than two years.

After the feasting was at an end, Captain Baggshaw gave us a description of the country to enable us to lay our plans accordingly. He said the nearest settlement was the town of St. Francisco, about forty miles north of our present encampment, situated on the south side of the Francisco Bay, formed by the river which we descended, which he calls Two Laries, or Bush River.[63] It is about three-fourths of a mile wide at its mouth, and is considered a safe harbor for almost any quantity of vessels; and within sixty or seventy miles south of us is the town of Monterey, also Spanish, the capital of this province, and which is called Upper California. He also informed us that about sixty or seventy miles north of St. Francisco, and about one hundred miles from our present position was a Russian settlement, which consists of about one hundred and fifty families who

63 The Tulare or San Joaquín River.

93

settled in this country a few years ago for the purpose of catching sea otter, which are of great value, on account of the quality of the fur. They also cultivate the ground to a considerable extent.[64] Captain Baggshaw went and examined the carcass of the whale which our men had found, and pronounced it to be the sperm whale, the oil of which is of the most valuable kind. He supposed it had been washed here when the sea was rough during a storm, and was unable to make its way back over the sand bars. From him, we also learned some further particulars concerning the mountain which had caused us so many hardships in crossing, parts of which were visible from the ocean, particularly the snow-covered peaks. This he called the California Mountain, as it runs parallel with the coast for a great distance, commencing at the mouth of the Columbia River, and extending along the coast to the mouth of Red River, or Gulf of California forming a beautiful country from the seashore to the base of the mountain, and extending north and south a distance of about six or seven hundred miles of rich soil, well timbered and abundantly watered by innumerable small streams heading in the mountain and flowing toward the Father of Waters.

Most of this vast waste of territory belongs to the Republic of the United States. What a theme to contemplate its settlement and civilization. Will the jurisdiction of the federal government ever succeed in civilizing the thousands of savages now roaming over these plains, and her hardy freeborn population here plant their homes, build their towns and cities, and say here shall the arts and sciences of civilization take root and flourish? Yes, here, even in this remote part of the great West before many years, will these hills and valleys be greeted with the enlivening sound, of the workman's hammer, and the merry whistle of the ploughboy. But this is left undone by the government, and will only be seen when too late to apply the remedy. The Spaniards are making inroads on the south—the Russians are encroaching with im-

[64] This was the settlement of the Russian-American Fur Company known as Fort Ross. It was established in 1812 and was sold to Captain John A. Sutter when the Russians abandoned California in 1842. Portions of the old fort are preserved.

punity along the seashore to the north, and further northeast the British are pushing their stations into the very heart of our territory, which, even at this day, more resemble military forts to resist invasion than trading stations. Our government should be vigilant. She should assert her claim by taking possession of the whole territory as soon as possible—for we have good reason to suppose that the territory *west* of the mountain will some day be equally as important to a nation as that on the *east*.[65]

The next day Captain Baggshaw took leave of us and started out on his trading expedition—appointing Monterey as the point where we were to meet in a few days.

The next morning after the departure of the ship, we were all in readiness to start for Monterey, the capital of the province, which lays in a southern direction. After traveling a few miles along the coast finding it very difficult in consequence of the wet, swampy ground, we found the carcass of another large fish, measuring forty-seven feet in length, with a horn or sword projecting from its nose twelve and one-half inches long. As traveling so near the water still continued difficult, we here concluded to strike out into the plain, where we found much better walking, the country being quite level, soil rich, and a few Indians. Some of these natives live well, as they cultivate pumpkins, beans, and some of them Indian corn—they also raise an abundance of melons, which grow to an enormous size. But all these Indians still seemed to be very ignorant and stupid.

On the evening of the 22d November we encamped at some rough hills near a small creek. In this neighborhood there are a great number of these hills, all of which are well covered with excellent timber, and abounding with all kinds of game except buffalo. The most of our company had become nearly barefooted for want of moccasins, as we had wore out everything of the kind in traveling from the Rocky Mountains—and, as winter was approaching, and no one knowing what kind of a reception we

[65] It is noteworthy that this need for urgency in American expansion westward to the Pacific was felt by a patriotic trapper-explorer more than a decade before the war with Mexico.

would meet with among the Spaniards, it was advised that we should tarry here and provide ourselves with an abundant winter supply of shoes. Accordingly, our hunters were despatched to scour these hills for the purpose of getting hides to make moccasins, &c., when we would be at leisure. In the evening the hunters all returned to camp, with the tongues of 93 deer and some of the hides, and also of some wild cattle, which are likewise very numerous. They brought the tongues in order to show the number each man had killed. The wild cattle are very timorous, keeping hid pretty much all day and feed at night. They are much wilder than deer, elk, &c. Our hunters brought in some of the choice parts of the cattle they had killed, which was quite fat beef, but it was much inferior to the meat of the buffalo of the Rocky Mountains. These cattle incline much to rough and hilly parts of the country, owing, it is supposed, to the Spaniards and Indians hunting them when found in the plains.

23d. This morning we directed our course across these hills. On arriving at the foot of the hills on the south side, we found one of the horns of these cattle which measured three and one-half feet on the outside or bend, and one foot in circumference at the root or thickest part. This we supposed had been the horn of an ox. These cattle are much larger and look better in their wild state than when domesticated. Their horns particularly are much larger than those of our country—but this is probably owing to the softness of the climate; as here there is no winter nor freezing weather. We continued across the plain and arrived on the banks of a small creek which empties into the sea at the distance of seven or eight miles, where we encamped for the night. Not long after we had halted, there was eight Spaniards arrived at our camp, from whom we found it as difficult to get information of any kind, as from most of the Indians. All our efforts to make them understand signs was unavailing, and not one of our company understood a word of Spanish. They were fine portly looking men, but looked as if they had been cast from civilized society as long as ourselves. They remained with us all night.

24th. We set out this morning for Monterey accompanied by the Spaniards as guides, who piloted us to the house of a Mr. Gibroy, who had been a brave and dutiful tar in his younger days, when he had learned to speak a little English. From this old man we gathered much useful information as to the country, climate, people, natives, &c. Here we concluded to remain for the night. The old man showed every disposition to give us all the information he could, and treated us very kindly.[66] We ascertained that we were within thirty-five miles of Monterey. In the morning we started in the direction of Monterey, intending to pass through the town of St. Juan or John which lay in the course we were going. Here we found the traveling much easier, as we now had some kind of roads to travel on, although they were far from being wagon roads—running through an extensive prairie of rich soil, with here and there a lonely hut built near some grove of timber or brook. Towards evening we arrived at St. Juan, which we now found to be a Spanish missionary station for the establishment of the Christian religion and civilization among the Indians.[67]

Here Captain Walker deemed it prudent to halt for a few days, in order to ascertain the disposition of the people, and make further inquiries with respect to the country, &c., lest we might be considered as intruders and treated in a way that we would not much like.[68] It was our desire to keep on peaceable terms with the Spaniards, at least no one desired to give the

[66] The Walker party had crossed the Santa Cruz Mountains into the Santa Clara Valley.

Scotch-born John Gilroy was the first foreigner to take up permanent residence in California. He was set ashore at Monterey from an English vessel, suffering from scurvy, in 1814 at the age of twenty. He was baptized at San Carlos (Carmel) Mission in 1814, and seven years later married the daughter of Ignacio Ortega. He was living with his wife on his San Isidro rancho at the time of the visit of the Walker party. Gilroy was a hard drinker and may have appeared much older than his forty years at that time. In later years he lost his land. He died in poverty in 1869. The town of Gilroy, Santa Clara County, stands on the site of his old rancho.

[67] This was the old mission of San Juan Bautista.

[68] Recalling the difficulties with Mexican officials experienced by Jedediah Smith on his two visits to California in the 1820's, Captain Walker was determined to establish friendly relations with both whites and Indians.

97

least offense of any kind—knowing that Spaniards and Indians had quite a different mode of carrying on warfare. We obtained privilege from the priests to select a convenient place for grass, wood, water, &c., to pitch our encampment, and immediately commenced erecting a breastwork, with which to defend ourselves in case we were attacked by Indians or anything else that chose to molest us. From information gained here, Captain Walker thought it advisable to go no further into their country, or the inhabited parts of it, owing to the difficulty in getting pasture for our horses and provisions for ourselves—as there is no preparations of any kind made for the accommodation of travelers; besides the expense of living would be much less to remain here where game was plenty and grass good.

Today Captain Walker, after getting a passport, which is necessary for a stranger to have in passing from one ward or district to another, and which must be renewed by the *alcalde* or squire in each district, took two men and started for Monterey,[69] where he intended presenting himself to the governor, and asking the permission of his excellency to pass the winter in his settlements, and to inform him where we were from, our business, intentions, &c.

St. Juan or St. John is beautifully situated on the banks of a small creek in a rich level plain, about twenty miles from the coast and about the same distance from Monterey, containing from six to seven hundred inhabitants—all of whom are Indians, with the exception of the priests and fifteen or twenty people who are occupied in teaching and instructing these heathens in the ways of religion and truth; besides giving them instructions in the art of farming and rendering the soil productive—with the hope that they will eventually succeed in inculcating into the minds of the savages such a knowledge of agriculture as will greatly conduce to the amelioration of the red man's condition. Their habitations are simple in construction—mostly such as may

[69] Monterey was both the capital of Upper California and its principal seaport at that time. It had a population of 708 men, women, and children in 1831. (Alexander Forbes, *California, a History of Upper and Lower California*, 102, 126.)

be found in the wildest parts of the mountains. But those of the missionary establishment are quite different, and plainly show the superiority of the white man over the Indian, both as regards comfort and convenience. This station much resembles a fort or garrison. The part which is called the church forms one side or end. The other three sides are divided into different departments like cells, each cell sheltering so many Indians, and covers near half an acre of ground, with the door of each cell opening to the inside. These buildings are the same as if they were under one roof, with the exception of a gate at each corner of the square. The buildings are constructed of brick, the principal part of which are dried in the sun. The walls are built thick and strong when built of this kind of brick. For rafters they use poles tolerably well shaped, and for lathing they make use of poles of a smaller size. The roof is generally composed of a kind of cane grass which is carefully laid on the rafters and then covered with earth for which purpose they generally have the roof nearly flat in order to hold the earth. But the church, or principal building, is built of handsome brick, and is well finished, being covered with tile. For the instruction of these Indians there is four hours of each day devoted to education and prayer, and the balance of the day is occupied in teaching them the rudiments of agriculture and the mechanical arts. The females are carefully instructed in the art of sewing and other accomplishments of housewifery. Everything in this station is under the control and management of the priests, who exercise the authority of governor, judge, &c., being privileged to try and condemn all criminal acts.[70]

On the first evening we spent in our new encampment, we were shown the manner in which the Spaniards take wild cattle, which was quite a different practice from that used by the Indians of the Rocky Mountains in taking buffalo, &c. Never less than two go at a time, who are always on the back of their fleetest

[70] San Juan Bautista was established by Father Junipero Serra in 1797 as a Franciscan mission station for the conversion and education of Indians. The settlement had a population of 987 in 1831. Historic buildings of this old mission fronting the plaza are still intact.

horses, each provided with a strong cord with a noose fixed on one end. When the animal is started they give chase and the rider that overtakes the game first, throws the noose round its neck or horns, and begins to draw the noose tight. When the noose is found to be secure he gives the cord several winds round the pummel of the saddle (which is made strong for this purpose) and stops his horse all of a sudden, which throws the animal to the ground and frequently breaks its neck. If the animal is thrown without injury, the other hunter comes forward with his noose and fastens it round its hind foot, which enables them to manage the stoutest and most ferocious bulls. Having thus captured their object of pursuit, they sometimes have great trouble in getting them home alive. The one with the cord round the animal's head goes before while he with the cord fastened to the hind foot stays in the rear. If their prisoner becomes refractory and refuses to advance, the man in the rear commences whipping, while he in front uses many devices to provoke the brute, until it in a fit of rage makes at him, when he puts off at full speed, and sometimes runs two or three miles in this way without stopping. In this manner they brought a large handsome cow into our camp this evening which we purchased, and found to be good beef.

Although they exhibit a great degree of dexterity in taking these wild beasts, their mode of killing them is far different. When they want to butcher their beef they make the horse with the noose round the neck pull a different way from the one with the noose round the foot, until the animal is thrown on the ground, when they dismount and cut its throat with large knives.

They appear to do most of their work on horseback. If they want wood they repair to the forest, ride along until they find a log to suit them, when they drop their noose round the end of it; and thus drag it to their homes. They are very expert on horseback, nor could it be otherwise, for they are constantly riding and never appear so well satisfied as when they are seated on a prancing steed.

On the first of December, Captain Walker returned from

Monterey, where he had met with a hospitable reception by the governor and principal people in and about the capital, and where he also again met with Captain Baggshaw, who served as an interpreter for Captain Walker and the governor, as he was fully capable of fulfilling such an office.[71] With the governor, Captain Walker succeeded in everything he desired, having obtained permission to remain in the country during the approaching winter, to hunt and kill as much game as would support our company, and to trade as much with the Spaniards as we pleased, but were forbid trapping in the Indian lands or trading with the natives. The Spaniards manifest a warm friendship for the Indian under their jurisdiction, as those who were friendly towards us were constantly reminding us of the danger of wronging the Indians.

Here we remained until about the 18th of December, without anything occurring except the daily visits we received from the Spaniards and Indians, who were curious to know how we lived, and all about us. They however, only found that we lived like they did themselves, any more than they lived in habitations built of wood, brick, mortar, &c., while we lived in huts made of skins of animals. About this time Captain Walker proposed to me to take a tramp through the settlements for the purpose of taking a view of the country, and the manners and customs of the inhabitants. This was precisely what I had long been wanting. Accordingly, Captain Walker, two others and myself left the camp and steered to the southeast, intending to return through Monterey. The country through which we passed contained rich soil, tolerably well timbered, but thinly inhabited with a few Spaniards and Indians, who appeared to live there because they were not permitted to live any other place. These people, generally, are very ignorant and much more indolent—have little or no ingenuity—and only seem to enjoy themselves

71 Walker approached the Mexican governor through an American sea captain as had Jedediah Smith, the first American explorer to reach California overland. However, Governor José Figueroa, who had taken office in 1833, was much more friendly toward foreigners than had been the Mexican authorities in Smith's time.

when engaged in the chase. This is the only occupation of the wealthier portion of Spaniards. Their habitations are built of sun-dried brick, some of which appear well enough on the outside, but the inside shows no kind of mechanism—there being no floor, partition, or work of any kind except the bare walls. Their floors are made smooth by taking a large beetle and hammering the surface of the ground until it becomes perfectly level —thus they never fail of having a solid foundation! They have a small fireplace in one corner of the house, with a chimney extending only a little above the mantle. Their beds and bedding generally consists of blankets spread upon a large hide laid on the ground, and after rising in the morning these beds are rolled up in one corner, where they answer the purpose of seats through the day time. Their diet is generally composed of beans and meat made into a kind of soup, with but little bread. Most of them are entirely destitute of cooking utensils, and, were it not that they are all provided with knives, their manner of cooking and eating would be equally as inconvenient as the wildest savages of the Rocky Mountains. But the wealthy, who, it may be supposed, constitute the aristocracy of this country, appear to live at ease, surrounded with all the comforts of life, are entirely independent and unconnected with the common people. They carry on farming to a considerable extent in some districts, the principal labor of which is done by the Indians from the missionary station. The principal productions are wheat, corn, and beans. They also have many vineyards, and manufacture a large quantity of wine—which is their principal drink. Their mode of preparing the soil for grain is of an awkward and rather novel nature. When they want to plough, they repair to the woods and get a sapling with a knot or branch jutting out on one side, which they make sharp, hitch two or more teams of oxen to it and then proceed to score out the ground—which is generally done in wet weather, when the ground is moist. Another method, no less novel, however, is to get a crooked log, much the shape of a sled-runner, fix a piece of iron in front which answers for a coulter, then sharpening the log they make a furrow similar to the track of a sled. As a substitute for a harrow, they use a brush, and by laying a weight on it, some times scratch the ground in tolerable style. This manner of tilling the soil could not be done with such success in any other country where the soil is less mellow and tender than here.

These people have no fences round their cleared or cultivated land, although they raise an immense amount of stock, such as horses, mules and horned cattle—all of which range at large over these extensive prairies all seasons of the year, many being in a manner totally wild, so much so that, when they wish to milk a cow, they mount one of their coarsers and noose her, fasten the cord to a tree, and then tie her feet, when she is forced to be quiet. During our whole stay in this country I have never seen anything like a stable or a barn, as a shelter for the dumb brutes —nor did I ever see anyone feeding an animal, unless it was a favorite cow or horse that was sick. This, however, is not at all singular as any number of animals could subsist, and be in good order all seasons of the year, on these plains, as in many spots the grass is green the whole year round. The months of August, September, and October are the least enticing to animals, as it is the warmest and driest season of the year. As soon as August sets in the beasts inhabiting the dry prairies and hills repair to the low wet ground, where they can get enough to subsist upon until the dry season passes away. The rainy season commences generally in the latter part of October, and continues until the first and sometimes middle of January, when the weather becomes fair and the farmers sow their grain, such as wheat and rye. During this wet weather the animals grow fat, and the inhabitants employ the principal part of this time in catching and domesticating them. This fair weather generally lasts about two months, or until the first of March, when the rain again descends and continues until about the middle of June—the grain, however, grows and ripens during the wet weather. It then keeps dry for a month or so until the farmers gather their crops—which occupies about a month, when the warm weather sets in, destroying all kinds of vegetation, giving but a poor subsistence to the dumb brutes, and to the country the appearance of an unproductive climate. About the end of the dry season (say about the first of November) the face of nature in this country has more the appearance of spring in the United States than any other part of the year, and, as there is no winter nor freezing weather here it may be said that August, September, and October is their only winter (to substitute *warm* for *cold*) as, at the end of this period the face of nature assumes a new dress and vegetation shoots forth precisely in the manner that it does in Pennsylvania when the frost leaves the ground in the spring of the year. The dry season is occupied by the inhabitants in gathering the mules into large droves and driving them off to the market at Santa Fe, a distance of twelve or fourteen hundred miles from this part of the coast, through a wild and desert country. Here they meet with ready sale at a profitable price from the traders of Missouri, who repair to Santa Fe annually for that purpose. These traders are generally well supplied with merchandise which they exchange at Santa Fe for gold and silver, and with these Californian traders for mules and Spanish hides. The price of a mule at Santa Fe is generally from six to ten dollars. Merchandise is sold at a great advance, particularly silks, jewelry, and groceries.[72]

The principal part of their hides are sold to U. S. vessels trading on the coast. When a trading vessel anchors on the coast for the purpose of trading, the news is spread over the whole country like wildfire. The owners of cattle, who are of the wealthier class, collect together all the poorer Spaniards and Indians for the purpose of catching and butchering the cattle, in order to get their hides. This is the commencement of their sporting season. They are all mounted on their fleetest horses, and on these occasions the hunters go in pairs, one provided with a noose and the other with a spear or lance, which is used in cutting the

[72] The best account of the Santa Fe trade is Josiah Gregg's *Commerce of the Prairies*, reprinted by the University of Oklahoma Press in 1954. See also Gregg's *Diary and Letters of Josiah Gregg* (Maurice Garland Fulton, ed.), first published by the same press in 1941 and 1944 (2 vols.).

sinews of the animals hind legs after it is noosed, which causes it to fall to the ground, after which they are easily despatched. After they strip off the hides and take out the tallow, and sometimes the choice part of the meat, the remainder of the carcass is left on the ground to be devoured by the wolves. The hides are then stretched out on the ground, and the tallow moulded into large cakes. As a compensation for their labor, the butchers, or hunters, receive one-third of all the tallow they can collect. When the vessel is about leaving the coast, the hides and tallow which has been collected, is conveyed to the beach, where the hides are sold at $1.50 apiece, and the tallow at four cents per pound.

The greater part of this cargo is paid for in merchandise at high prices, but which is as valuable here as money itself, and much more useful. A vessel loaded with hides and tallow from this coast is of the greatest value, and has afforded an easy path to wealth for many of the American merchants.[73]

After traveling leisurely along through their country, which still continued thinly inhabited by these people, and passing two small missionary establishments, we arrived at a small town called St. Jose, or St. Joseph, about ten miles south of Monterey, where we arrived on the 25th of December. This is also a missionary station, and the largest of any we had yet encountered, containing about nine hundred Indians, principally from the mountains. This station is constructed and managed similar to that of St. Juan, except the church, which is much larger, and built with a greater display of the arts of civilization. Here we remained for two days, employing our time in watching the proceedings of these Indians in their devotional exercises. The manoeuvres of those who have been lately converted to the Christian religion (being of the Catholic faith) is something very singular, as they at one moment manifest the most unbounded transports of joy, and the next throw themselves into the greatest

---

[73] The classic description of the hide and tallow trade by American vessels on the California coast is Richard H. Dana's *Two Years Before the Mast.* Dana was on the coast in 1835.

paroxysms of weeping and lamentation.[74] We then continued our journey and soon arrived at Monterey, which town is built on a beautiful situation on the south side of Monterey Bay—this bay being formed by Kings River. This is the capital of Upper, or North California, and under the government of New Mexico. The town is small containing only about thirty or forty dwelling houses, one church, one calaboose, a part of which is used as a house of justice, or in other words, a court house, where the governor transacts his public business, and a kind of a fort, built in a commanding situation on the edge of the bay, to be used in the defense of the town in case an attack should be made upon it from the sea, containing several pieces of artillery.

This bay is very deep, affording an excellent harbor for any number of vessels. The town has every natural advantage that a seaport could desire; and if a proper spirit of enterprise prevailed among the inhabitants, it might be made to flourish equal to any other town in the dominion of New Mexico. Vessels sailing along the coast of the Pacific to the north, all stop here to take in supplies, as it is the last white settlement they pass until they reach the Russian dominions of the Northwest;[75] but as the inhabitants raise no grain only what is used for home consumption; the mariner is only enabled to supply his vessel with meat and water. Besides the advantage the agriculturalist might derive by supplying vessels with provisions, he might be enabled to carry on a large exporting business—as the soil and climate is every calculated to raise large crops of grain. Another prominent advantage the town of St. Joseph would have, is the facility of

[74] This was not the Mission San José but Mission San Carlos Borromea, which was founded by Father Serra on June 3, 1770, at Monterey. It was moved to this site in the fertile valley of the Carmel River in 1771. In 1831 this station had a population of 236. Captain William Smyth's watercolor shows this mission when it was at its height in 1827, and before the secularization of the missions had begun in 1831. Father Junipero Serra, founder of the Franciscan missions of California, is buried beneath the sanctuary of the church.

[75] Leonard had not visited San Francisco and did not mention it. The harbor at Monterey was only an open bay or roadstead, inferior to the sheltered bay of San Francisco. Alexander Forbes (*California*, 102) recognized that the port of San Francisco would be superior to that of Monterey for the foreign commerce of California.

106

internal communication with the Indians now inhabiting the prairies and mountains of the interior, or the white race, who, it may reasonably be expected, will have undisputed dominion over this entire region before long.

As it is at present, there are some men here of considerable wealth, the principal part of which they have acquired by trading with vessels different kinds of peltries, such as Spanish hides, tallow, beaver, sea otter, bear, deer, and elk skins, and also horses and mules. There is also a brisk trade carried on in this place with the Sandwich Islands, about nine day sail from this port, and which might be rendered quite lucrative. The most of the vessels, however that put into this bay are on fishing expeditions. The sperm whale are very numerous in this part of the Pacific Ocean—the oil of which affords a profitable reward to all who embark in this dangerous and toilsome business.

On the 29th some of our men arrived in St. Joseph,[76] with a portion of the peltries we had collected whilst crossing the mountains, and which we exchanged with Captain Baggshaw for merchandise, such as groceries and ammunition to do us whilst on our return to Missouri the next summer. After concluding our trade with Captain Baggshaw, and spending the last day of the expiring year on land, we all resolved by invitation, to celebrate New Year's day on board the *Lagoda*, with the governor and Captain Baggshaw. The day was spent quite merrily, and the whole company manifested the best possible humor, each one contributing to keep up the sport by telling some mountain adventure or seafaring exploit. In the evening we ended the celebration by returning on shore and taking a few rounds with our rifles—which terminated by conclusively convincing the sailors that if they could beat us in telling "long yarns," we were more than a match for them with the rifle.

On the morning of the 2d of January, 1834, Captain Baggshaw insisted on us again visiting his vessel, for the purpose of taking a glass, which we gladly accepted, and after shaking hands all round, and affectionately bidding farewell with our friends

[76] Leonard meant Monterey and not St. Joseph.

on board the vessel, returned to land in company with the governor, when his excellency offered our Captain a gratuity of a tract of land seven miles square if he would bring fifty families, composed of different kinds of mechanics, and settle on it. Captain Walker was well pleased with the country, and said he had a great mind to accept the governor's offer, as he had no doubt he could in a few years amass a fortune, and be at the head of a rich and flourishing settlement; but his love for the laws and free institutions of the United States, and his hatred for those of the Spanish government, deterred him from accepting the governor's benevolent offer—and we bid farewell to the governor and his people, well pleased with the reception we had thus far everywhere met with among the Spaniards.

We now left St. Joseph and returned with our merchandise, consisting principally of groceries, ammunition, &c., to our encampment, where we arrived without meeting with any difficulty; finding everything in good order, and all well except one man named Philips, who was laying in a very precarious state from wounds inflicted by a bear. It appeared that Philips had been out hunting deer, and having killed one, took out the insides and hung it upon a tree, and started to the camp to get a horse to bring it home. After traveling a mile or so, whilst ascending a hill, came suddenly upon an old bear and two cubs. The bear immediately on seeing Philips, as is their custom, reared on her hind feet, and being very close, commenced growling most furiously. This our hero could not brook, and fearing the consequences if he should shoot and wound her, lost his presence of mind and started to run. The bear immediately pursued and caught him. He now found it quite useless to attempt to get loose, and only saved his life by sinking to the ground and affecting to be dead. The bear then left him, but not without wounding him to such a degree that it was a long time before he could collect strength enough to raise to his feet. It was late at night when he reached the camp, and was so far gone, from hunger and loss of blood, that his life was despaired of at first. One of his arms was broke and his body most shockingly cut and mangled.

Early View of the Yosemite Valley

By T. A. Ayres, 1859

National Park Service

The Giant Redwoods

Startling and Already Old When Zenas Leonard Saw Them

On our way from the capital to our camp, we had an opportunity of witnessing a part of the Spanish mode of gambling in this country, which was rare amusement to us, and which they call bull-baiting. It is in this fashion, as near as I could understand: When a number of sporting gentlemen get together for this purpose, they repair to the prairies, all well mounted and prepared for the chase. When they come across a herd of cattle they make large bets on who shall be the first to noose one of the cattle in the drove in sight. When everything is arranged this far, they all take an even start. The one that gets the rope round the animal's horn or neck first claims the assistance of the rest to throw the animal to the ground—which ends the chase for this time. As the Spaniards are generally skilled in the art of throwing the noose, the chase in a case of this kind mostly depends on the fleetness of the horses. When they have secured a bull in this way, they take him to a pen made strong for this purpose, where they put him in for safe-keeping, and settle the bets. Having got through with this game, to give the losers an opportunity to regain their losses, they start out on the hunt of a grizzly bear, always preferring the largest, which they capture in the same way. Taking a bear is a much more dangerous piece of work, than any other animal, owing to their enormous strength. It often happens that, in taking a bear, they are unhorsed; when, if alone, they are in imminent danger of being tore to pieces; but this seldom happens unless the horse is thrown, or the saddle tore loose. In taking a bear, their object is to noose him round one of the hind legs, in order to keep him from biting the cord, which they are very apt to do if fast round the neck. A single hunter can do but little with a large bear, and they are seldom attacked single handed, or without the certainty of assistance from some of their comrades. When overtaken by the foremost rider, the bear stops running and prepares for war. This man will then engage the attention of the bear by teasing him, whilst another hunter will come up in the rear of the excited animal and noose him by the hind foot; when the cord is securely fastened to the hind foot, he is generally considered safe. It is then that their sport begins in good earnest, and the feats that are sometimes performed by the men, bear, and horses, would be incredible to any person who has never seen any sport of this kind. After the bear finds himself secure and has become pretty well worried, he seats himself sullenly on the ground and lets the horse pull at the cord, stretching his leg out until the pain becomes too severe, when he will draw up his leg, horse and all, with as much apparent ease as a horse would a sleigh. I have been told that some of the largest bears have been known to drag two horses a considerable distance in a fit of rage, in spite of all the exertions of the horses and riders to the contrary. After the bear is pretty well worried in this way, another noose is fastened round one of the fore feet or neck, when the bear will commence beating the ground with his feet and manifesting the most intense rage and anger imaginable— and in this manner they drag, whip, and coax him along to the pen where the bull is confined.

Their cords are made of green cowhide, which they cut into narrow strips, hang them in the sun, and rub them as they dry, making them soft and pliable, when they are plaited into a rope which no weight can sever.

When the bear has arrived at the bull pen, their bets on taking him and all disputes are settled, refreshments taken, and preparations made for another scene, which is by far the most pleasing to the Spaniards. They begin to enrage the bull by pricking him with a nail fixed in the end of a stick, and when his anger has rose to the war pitch, the bear is let into the pen with the bull. The men now bet all they are worth on which will be the conqueror, and everything manifests the greatest possible excitement. Sometimes the animals refuse to fight until they are forced to it by being tormented with the sharpened sticks, but when one receives a blow from the other, nothing can part them until one or the other falls. These fights last sometimes half an hour without relaxation. The bear is much the strongest, but it has no chance of avoiding the thrusts of the bull, in consequence of the smallness of the pen; but in an open field, a grizzly bear will conquer a bull in a few moments.

When the fight is over the conquered animal is taken out and the bets are again settled. If it is the bear that is whipt, the game is continued and the bets renewed on some person who will offer to go into the pen with the enraged bull, lay his hand on some part of his body, and escape untouched. This is by far the most dangerous part of the whole play, and many lives have been lost at it; but so fond are the Spaniards of gambling, that in play a life is of but little consequence. When the bets are all arranged, the adventurer stands at the door of the pen with his blanket in his hand, and the company is occupied in maddening the bull. When he has become sufficiently enraged the hero steps in, when the bull will make a desperate plunge at him with his horns, which the man escapes by throwing the blanket over the face of the bull and blinding him—he then claps his hand on the designated spot, snatches the blanket off his horns and makes his escape. If he gets out without the bull striking him, he has won the stakes for all those who bet on him—which will be a profitable business for him, as he receives a certain percentage on all the money thus won.

It happened that one of these games was to be played while we were in the neighborhood, and on being invited to attend Captain Walker, several others, and myself concluded on going to see the performance. When we reached the ground the Spaniards had the bull and the bear both secured, and were just going to set them to fighting. Presently the animals got to blows, and continued for a short time, when the bull became master and the bear was let out of the pen. The battle was very closely contested, and I never seen animals so much enraged, and fight with so much fierceness. The bear could master the bull for a good spell, when it could get its arms around him, but the large body of the bull would prevent any serious injury, and presently the bear would be shaken to the ground, when the bull would have a chance to plunge at him with effect. It was in this manner that the bull managed to get the advantage of bruin. After the bear was taken out, the company commenced betting on an old time-worn Spaniard who offered to go into the pen and touch the enraged animal. In a short time all the preliminaries were arranged, and the man entered the pen in the manner as described above, but unfortunately, when he went to pull his blanket off the animal's head and come out, one of the beast's horns was thrust quite through his thigh. As soon as this happened, the Spaniards commenced plaguing the bull at the opposite side of the pen and the wounded man was suffered to crawl out in the best manner he could.

There are also many other methods of gambling practiced by these people, and vice of every description seems to be openly countenanced in some parts of the settlements, such as horse racing, card playing, and even stealing. The latter of which is carried on to a considerable extent by both male and female, and is even recognized, under some circumstances, as one of the established customs of the country. The men are always provided with dirks, which they can use with superior skill.

We remained at our old encampment near St. Juan, without meeting with any thing to disturb our situation, and on the most friendly intercourse with both Spaniards and Indians, until last night, when six of our best horses were stolen, and which we at first supposed to be the work of Indians. We had heretofore trusted everything in the fidelity of both the Spaniards and Indians, but when our horses had been thus taken from us we began to keep a sharp look out. In the morning (10th) several scouting parties were despatched in search of the stolen property, and returned in the evening with only one, after following the trail far into the Spanish settlement, which convinced us immediately that it was not the Indians but the Spaniards who had behaved so dishonorable. In the following morning Captain Walker went himself to one of the *alcaldes* or esquires for the purpose of enquiring what steps had best be taken to restore our stolen property, or how we could be recompensed. On having an interview with the magistrate he learned a good many things more than he had formerly known—which was this, that Spaniards, whilst traveling through the country with a poor horse, was at liberty to take a good one if he could find such, no matter who it belonged to, or whether wild or tame, and continue his journey. And also, if two men set down to play at cards, and the loser thinks that his opponent has cheated or defrauded him, he is at liberty to visit his horses and help himself to such as he can, but if the owner catches him in the act, it generally ends in bloodshed. For this and other reasons, a Spaniard is never seen away from home without his rope or cord, in order to noose anything he stands in need of.

Stealing horses is practiced more than any other kind of theft, and it is not recognized as a crime, owing, probably, to the cheapness of these animals—as they can be bought at any time for from one to ten dollars. Those costing one dollar are unbroke fillies, and those for ten dollars are first rate horses well tamed. When we became aware that such was the practice of the country, Captain Walker thought it would be the best plan for us to pack up and leave the neighborhood, in order to avoid a difficulty with a people of a ferocious and wicked nature, at a time too, when we were not very well prepared to contend against such an enemy in their own country. Accordingly we set about purchasing provision, and the next day we were pretty well supplied with flour, corn, beans, &c.

13th. This morning everything was prepared and we took up our march in an eastern direction.[77] We only traveled twelve or fifteen miles this day and encamped for the night, which we spent without the occurrence of anything of importance more than the recalling to mind of the scenes encountered and hardships endured by each of us in our wayfaring to this remote corner of the world.

The two following days we continued without interruption in the same direction, and encamped on the banks of a beautiful stream called Sulphur River, where we concluded to remain until

[77] Watson (*West Wind*, 66) gave the date January 13, 1834, for the Walker party's departure from San Juan Bautista on its eastward march.

in the spring, when it would be more pleasant traveling eastward to the Rocky Mountains. Our encampment is beautifully located on a rising piece of ground, with a handsome river gliding smoothly along immediately in front, an extensive oat plain stretching out as far as the eye will reach to the rear, and is about forty miles east of St. Juan. The banks of this river are most delightfully shaded with timber, principally oak and elm. The soil in the plain is very strong and deep, producing heavy crops of wild oats and grass—affording excellent pasture for horses, at this season of the year.

After we had made every arrangement necessary to our comfort while we remained here, our men commenced hunting in good style—bear, elk, and deer being very plenty, and the fattest we had anywhere met with. On the 20th, it being a fine day for hunting, a large portion of our sportsmen set out early in the morning bound for a general hunt, and determined to rake the whole prairie. Towards the middle of the day, two of the men came in sight of a large drove of elk, feeding in the open prairie, and as they were continuously approaching near enough to shoot, they unexpectedly came upon five grizzly bear that were sleeping in the grass—two old ones and three cubs; the latter began to howl most piteously, which enraged the old ones, and they made at our hunters with open mouth. But as one of them was an old practitioner in such matters, having a good gun, carrying an ounce ball, which he called *"Knock-him-stiff,"* stood quite composed (bidding his companion, who was about to run, to stand his ground) until the bear came within reach of him when he discharged it with the muzzle in her mouth —which, as our hero said, gave her a very bad cough. This inspired the other hunter with courage, and he treated the other bear in nearly the same manner. The cubs not showing any desire to depart alone, were also killed. This day's hunt was exceedingly lucky, not only to these two men, but to nearly all who were out, as they all returned with heavy loads of game.

On the 25th Captain Walker started to Monterey with eight men for the purpose of laying in a larger supply of provision for us on our journey to the east, in the spring, as we began to reflect that we might fall in with some other companies on the road who would need assistance.

26th. Today about 10 o'clock, we discovered a large drove of horses passing through the plain, followed by a few people, whom we supposed to be Spaniards or Indians—but they did not appear to know that we were in the neighborhood, and we were not anxious to let them know it for fear they might *travel* our way some time. In the evening, as some of our men who had been out hunting, were returning home, they accidentally came across a large bear laying in a hole, sound asleep. Our men were anxious to see some sport, and commenced making a noise, and even fired a gun or two without bringing her to her senses and getting her out of the hole. They then dismounted, stationed themselves around the hole and shot her before she moved. On examination, they found her to be of the grizzly species and of the largest size; and also having two young ones in the hole with her, not larger than a common sized cat. The old one was extremely fat, and from the signs about the hole, it appeared that she must have had this as a permanent place of residence. It is the first instance I ever knew of taking a bear of this size whilst asleep.

28th. Today a party of Spaniards arrived at our encampment in search of a party of Indians who had eloped from the St. Juan missionary station, and taken with them three hundred head of horses—which we supposed to be the party seen by us on the 26th. These men stayed with us all night and the next morning some of our men joined the Spaniards in the chase, who were to get one-half of the horses as a compensation for their trouble, if lucky enough to find them. These men followed the Indians to the foot of a large mountain, where they discovered several smokes rising out of the forest along the base of the mountain. In a thicket of timber, from that smoke that arose, they thought the whole Indian force was concentrated, and the Spanish and American force surrounded the spot in battle array, determined to give the offenders a severe chastisement at once.

When all the preparations were made, the word to fire was given. But instead of the lamentations of wounded Indians, and the frantic prancing of frightened horses, nothing but a dead silence answered the discharge of their artillery. They then dismounted and went into the thicket, where they found a large portion of their horses well butchered, and partly dried and a few old and feeble Indians, with some squaws and children. The Indians having killed some of the horses, were engaged in drying the meat, but on seeing the white men approach, fled to the mountain, leaving nothing behind but what is above stated. The disappointment of the Spaniards now exceeded all bounds, and gave our men some evidence of the depravity of the Spanish character. By way of revenge, after they found that there was no use in following the Indians into the mountain, the Spaniards fell to massacring, indiscriminately, those helpless creatures who were found in the wigwams with the meat, and cutting off their ears. Some of them were driven into a wigwam, when the door was barricaded, and a large quantity of combustible matter thrown on and around the hut, for the purpose of setting fire to it, and burning them all together. This barbarous treatment our men would not permit and they went and released the prisoners, when the Spaniards fell to work and despatched them as if they were dogs. When this tragedy was completed they all returned to our encampment on the 31st.

On their arrival at our camp, the Spaniards told me that their object in taking off the ears was to show the priests and *alcaldes*, that they had used every effort to regain the stolen property. These people also informed me that the Indians of this country are in the habit of coming in large droves to the missionary stations, and make the most sincere professions of religion, until they gain the confidence of the priests, when they will suddenly decamp, and take off all the horses they can get, to the mountain, where they remain as long as their meat lasts—when they will send another detachment, whose duty it is to do likewise. They prefer eating domesticated horses because the act of stealing them gives their flesh a superior flavor—and it would be less trouble for them to catch wild horses, if they could thus gratify their stealing propensities.

There is supposed to be about ten Indians to one white man, or Spaniard, in this country. The population is divided or classed into three degrees. 1st. The whites or Spaniards. 2nd. The Indians; and third the offspring of a white and an Indian. The seasons are distinguished only as *wet* and *dry*—there being no snow and very little frost. The only established religion is that of the Roman Catholic faith, which is professed by almost every Spaniard.

Today Captain Walker returned from the settlements well supplied with such articles as he was in need of—bringing with him one hundred horses, forty-seven cow cattle, and thirty or thirty-five dogs, together with some flour, corn, beans, &c., suitable for our subsistence in the long journey, for which every man was now busily engaged in making preparations. Two or three days after Captain Walker returned from this expedition, we were visited by forty or fifty Spaniards, all well mounted, and each man prepared with a noose, on their way into the neighborhood of wild horses, for the purpose of catching some. In this company we found one of the horses which had been stolen from us before we left the settlement. The Spaniards honorably gave him up after we proved our claim. As the manner of taking wild horses was altogether a curiosity to me, I was anxious to see the sport, and accordingly several others and myself joined the Spaniards and accompanied them. After traveling a short distance we arrived at a large pen, enclosing about three-fourths of an acre, which they call a park or correll. This pen is built quite strong, to prevent horses from breaking through. Attached to this pen, are two wings extending to the right and left, in the shape of a V, upwards of a mile and a half in length. The wings are made by posts being set in the ground and poles tied to them with a piece of elk or horse hide, about four feet high— the neck or pen being built much higher and stronger. This pen appears as if it had been used for this purpose many years. After we halted here, the Spaniards were occupied during the re-

117

mainder of the day in repairing some weak parts of the pen and wings, and in the morning all hands proceeded to drive in the horses, which was done by sending out parties in different directions, mounted upon the swiftest horses in order to outrun the wild ones and turn them in front of the pen, when the men all collect in a breast and drive them down into the pen; which answers the same purpose as a basket does a fish-dam. When the animals are all in the pen, a fence is erected across the neck to prevent the escape of any horses. The men will then dismount and pass along close to the pen for the purpose of accustoming the horses to the smell of human beings. When this is done, four or five will enter the pen, leaving the balance on the outside to prevent them from breaking out, and with their cords noose and tie all under two or three years old. After securing seventy or eighty in this manner, all over this age were turned out, as they are considered too hard to tame. They then blind-folded those they had taken and turned them loose with the tame horses, and they followed the same as a dog. It is in this way they always get them into the settlements, where they are divided to each man, who brands and hobbles them, and then turns them loose upon the prairie. After they have been confined in this situation two or three days, they are considered domesticated, their fetters taken off, and treated similar to the other horses.

There is another way of catching these horses, which is this: They are noosed, thrown to the ground, partly blindfolded, and saddled, when some adventurous Spaniard will mount on his back, let the horse rise to his feet, and if he becomes unmanageable, they give him the whip, and run the brute until he is no longer able to keep his feet under him, after which he is generally sufficiently docile.

On the 12th we returned to our camp, when Captain Walker traded with the Spaniards for several of these horses—and in the evening they bid us farewell and continued their homeward journey.

Feb. 14th. This morning had been appointed for our departure, and accordingly everything requisite for our comfort was in readiness, and we lazily left our camp for the east—leaving six of our company behind, all of whom are tradesmen, such as carpenters, hatters, &c., where they purposed following their occupations, which will no doubt be profitable to themselves, and of great advantage to the indolent and stupid Spaniard.[78] The price of furniture here is exceedingly high. A rough table (more like a bench) consisting of rough hewn boards nailed together, will cost eight and ten dollars. A pair of similar made bedsteads the same. Two of our men constructed a windmill which they sold for $110. All kinds of mechanical productions command a corresponding price. This is partly owing to the inconvenience of getting out the stuff—there being no saw-mills in the country, the carpenter is compelled to cut out his stuff by hand; and as there are very few tools in the country, it requires great labor to manufacture a piece of work with any kind of taste.

The parting scene between the company and these six men appeared the most melancholy separation we had undergone since we left the States. On other occasions, when we had separated with a portion of our hunters, it was with the confident hope of meeting again. But these men remained with the determination of making a permanent residence in the country, and never again returning to the states; whilst the most of us were as determinedly bent on never again returning to this region— hence we parted as if we were forever afterwards to be separated by worlds. On shaking hands with these men, with whom I had been in daily intercourse for the last eighteen months, it appeared more like parting with brothers, than anything else.

Our company was now reduced to 52 men, 315 horses—and for provisions, 47 beef, and 30 dogs, together with a considerable portion of flour, Indian corn, beans, some groceries, and a few other articles necessary on such an expedition. We continued up Sulphur River in an eastern direction, and for the first night encamped on the south side of this stream, after traveling not more than twelve or fifteen miles.

[78] George Nidever and John Price were two of the six members of the Walker party who remained in California.

119

15th. Continued our journey up Sulphur River,[79] passing through a fine country, most of which is prairie, covered plentifully with wild oats and grass. After we had encamped this evening, two Spaniards came to our camp bringing with them twenty-five very fine horses, which they sold to the company, and engaged themselves to accompany us to the buffalo country. They informed us that they had deserted from the Spanish army, and that as it was the second time, if taken now, according to the Spanish military discipline, their punishment would be certain death.

We continued traveling from day to day, the country all the way being of the most enticing nature, soil very strong, timber tolerably plenty, and game in abundance. The two Spaniards we found to be of great advantage to us, as some of our horses caused us great trouble, and one of the Spaniards being an excellent rider and well acquainted with the art of noosing, would catch and bring together our horses at any time they would become separated.

About the 27th we arrived at the base of the California Mountain, having passed many Indians on our way, and also finding many here.

On the 28th we continued our journey to the south along the base of the mountain in search of pasture for our cattle and a convenient pass over the mountain. Here game is very scarce, owing to the numerous swarms of Indians scattered along in every direction. On the second of March we killed one of our beef. Pursued our course, still in a southern direction finding game rather scarce, Indians plenty, pasture improving, and vegetation of every description beginning to grow rapidly— weather showery with warm sun, until the 10th of March, when we arrived at sixty or seventy huts, containing from two hundred and fifty to three hundred Indians. These Indians appear quite different from those more convenient to the Spanish settlements, and call themselves Pagans, their chief Capetaine, and have

[79] Leonard's "Sulphur River" is the San Joaquín. The party had crossed the Diablo Range into the broad valley of the San Joaquín.

names for several things nearly the same as we have. Their wives they call wifa—kettle, wood, and meat the same as we do. These people seem to live poor, and are equally as indolent as any of those we had met with in the Spanish dominions. They are generally small in stature, complexion quite dark, and some quite hairy. Whilst here we killed another of our beef, and made a present of some of the beef, together with a dog and some tobacco, to these Indians. Their principal diet during this season of the year consists of roots and weeds, amongst which is parsly, and a kind of cabbage, all of which they eat raw. In the summer they subsist principally upon acorns, at least a person would so judge to see the number of holes that are burnt into the logs for the purpose of mashing them.

When we were leaving these Indians, their chief brought a hearty and good-looking young female to our captain and proposed to give her in exchange for an ox. Captain Walker very prudently declined the offer, telling the chief that we had a great distance to travel, and would probably be without meat half the time. We traveled along quite comfortably, meeting with no unusual occurrence. The country through which we passed still continued as charming as the heart of man could desire. The Indians were quite numerous, some of whom would at times manifest the most unbounded alarm. We also passed a great number of streams flowing out of the mountain, and stretching afar toward the Pacific. The prairies were most beautifully decorated with flowers and vegetation, interspersed with splendid groves of timber along the banks of the rivers—giving a most romantic appearance to the whole face of nature.

We at length arrived at an Indian village, the inhabitants of which seemed to be greatly alarmed on seeing us, and they immediately commenced gathering up their food and gathering in their horses—but as soon as they discovered that we were white people, they became perfectly reconciled. After we halted here we found that these people could talk the Spanish language, which we thought might be of great advantage to the company, and on inquiry ascertained that they were a tribe called the

Concoas, which tribe some eight or ten years since resided in the Spanish settlements at the misionary station near St. Barbara, on the coast, where they rebelled against the authority of the country, robbed the church of all its golden images and candle-sticks, and one of the priests of several thousand dollars in gold and silver, when they retreated to the spot where we found them—being at least five or six hundred miles distant from the nearest Spanish settlement. This tribe are well acquainted with the rules of bartering for goods or anything they wish to buy—much more so than any other tribe we met with. They make regular visits to such posts where they are unknown, and also make appointments with ship-traders to meet at some designated time and place; thus they are enabled to carry on a considerable degree of commerce. They still retain several of the images which they pilfered from the church—the greater part of which is the property of the chiefs. These people are seven or eight hundred strong, their houses are constructed of poles and covered with grass, and are tolerably well supplied with household furniture which they brought with them at the time they robbed the church. They follow agricultural pursuits to some extent, raising very good crops of corn, pumpkins, melons, &c. All the out-door labor is done by the females. They are also in the habit of making regular visits to the settlements for the purpose of stealing horses, which they kill and eat.

We passed one night with these Indians, during which time they informed us of an accessible passage over the mountain. In the morning we resumed our journey, hiring two of these Indians as pilots, to go with us across the mountain—continued all day without any interruption, and in the evening encamped at the foot of the passover.[80]

In the morning we continued up the mountain in an eastern direction, and encamped this evening at the lower end of the snow. The next day we found the snow more plenty, and en-

[80] Watson (*West Wind*, 69) traced the route of the Walker party up Kern River to the summit of the Sierra Nevada Range. The Indians met along this route probably were Tubatulabels ("Pine-nut Eaters"), Shoshonean-speaking people.

camped without grass of any kind. We now began to apprehend hard times again. Our horses no longer resumed their march in the mornings with a playful cheerfulness, but would stumble along and go just when their riders would force them to do so. We continued traveling in this way for four days when we landed safely on the opposite side of the mountain, in a temperate climate, and among tolerable pasture, which latter was equally as gratifying to our horses as the former was to the men.[81]

We here made our pilots presents of a horse, some tobacco, and many trifling trinkets captivating to the eye of an Indian, when they left us to return to their friends.

Our horses and cattle were pretty much fatigued, but not as much as we anticipated. The country on this side is much inferior to that on the opposite side—the soil being thin and rather sandy, producing but little grass, which was very discouraging to our stock, as they now stood in great want of strong feed. On the opposite side vegetation had been growing for several weeks—on this side, it has not started yet.

After discharging our pilots we traveled a few miles and encamped at some beautiful springs, where we concluded to spend the remainder of the day, in order to give our horses and cattle rest. Our Captain here concluded on following the base of the mountain to the north until we would come to our trail when crossing to the west, or California.[82]

May 2nd. This morning we resumed our journey, every man possessed of doubtful apprehensions as to the result of this determination, as the hardships which we encountered in this region on a former occasion, were yet fresh in the minds of many of us. The country we found to be very poor, and almost entirely destitute of grass. We continued through this poor country trav-

[81] The eastbound crossing of the Sierras was made at a considerably lower altitude and with much less difficulty than had been the party's westward crossing of the range farther north. The route taken in the return crossing has been known since that time as Walker Pass, in honor of the leader of this expedition. It has an elevation of 5,245 feet.

[82] East of the mountains, the party turned northward and probably proceeded through the present Owens Valley.

eling a few miles every day, or as far as the weakened state of our dumb brutes would admit of. The weather was mostly clear and otherwise beautiful, but we had quite a cold wind most all the time. Traveling along the eastern base of this (California) Mountain, we crossed many small rivers flowing towards the east, but emptying into lakes scattered through the plain, or desert, where the water sinks and is exhausted in the earth. This plain extends from here to the Rocky Mountains, being an almost uninterrupted level, the surface of which is covered with dry, loose sand.

In this manner we traveled along, passing such scenes as are described above, until at length we arrived at some springs which presented a really remarkable appearance, and may be called boiling, or more properly Steam Springs, situated near the base of the mountain, on or near the banks of a small river. These springs are three in number, and rise within a short distance of each other, one being much larger than the other two. The water constantly boils as if it was in a kettle over a fire, and is so hot that if a piece of meat is put under the water at the fountain-head, it will cook in a few minutes, emitting a strong sulphurous smell—the water also tastes of sulphur. In a clear morning the steam or smoke rising from these springs may be seen a great distance as it hangs in the air over the springs, similar to a dense sheet of fog. There is not a spear of vegetation growing within several rods of the spot, and the surface of the ground presents the appearance of one solid piece of crust, or hard baked mud. When the water empties in and mixes with the river water, it leaves an oily substance floating on the surface similar to tar or grease of any kind.

About the 25th of May, we again continued our journey, but our difficulties had been multiplying for some time, until now we found them quite formidable. The principal part of our present difficulties arose from the scarcity of pasture for our horses and cattle. After traveling the best way we could, for a few days towards the north, we arrived at another beautiful sandy plain, or desert, stretching out to the east far beyond the reach of the

Original Water Color, Peabody Museum, Harvard

Mission San Carlos, California

As Seen by Captain William Smyth, 1822

From a lithograph in Forbes, *History of Upper and Lower California*, 1839

Monterey, Capital of Upper California

By Captain William Smyth, 1822

eye, as level as the becalmed surface of a lake. We occasionally found the traces of Indians, but as yet, we have not been able to gain an audience with any of them, as they flee to the mountain as soon as we approach. Game being very scarce, and our cattle poor, gives us very indifferent living.

Our direct course, after reaching the eastern base of this mountain, would have been a northeast direction, but we were apprehensive of perishing for water in crossing this extensive desert—which would doubtless be the fate of any traveler who would undertake it, when it is recollected that it extends from the base of the Rocky Mountains to this mountain, a distance of several hundred miles. This being the case we were obliged to pass along the base of the mountain in a northern direction, until we would arrive at the point where we ascended the mountain when going to the coast, and then follow the same trail east towards the Rocky Mountains, or Great Salt Lake, where we expected to meet the company we had left at the latter place. Traveling along the mountain foot, crossing one stream after another, was anything but pleasant. Day after day we traveled in the hope each day of arriving at the desired point when we would strike off in a homeward direction. Every now and then some of the company would see a high peak or promontory, which he would think was seen by the company on a former occasion, but when we would draw near to it our pleasing anticipations would be turned into despondency; and at one time, about the middle of May, our Captain was so certain that he could see a point in the distance, which he had distinctly marked as a guide on our former tramp, that he ordered the men to prepare for leaving the mountain; this also proved to be the result of imagination only.

The next morning our Captain, thinking the desert not very wide at this point, decided on striking across in a northeastern direction, which would shorten our route considerably, if we could only be so successful as to surmount the difficulties of traveling through loose sand, without water (as the streams descending from the mountain into the plain all sink).

On the 10th of May, everything necessary for our dry tramp

125

being in readiness, we started across the plain, which was done with a willing heart by almost every man, as we were all anxious to get home, and had been traveling many days without getting any nearer. The traveling in the plain, after passing the termination of the streams, we found to be extremely laborious. The sand lays quite loose, and as the wind would blow whilst driving our horses and cattle ahead of us, the sand would be raised up in such clouds that we could scarcely see them, which was very painful to our eyes. The first night in the plain we encamped at a large hole or well dug deep in the ground, which we supposed to be the work of Indians, and in which we found a small portion of stagnant water, but not half enough to slake the thirst of our numerous herd.

The next morning we resumed our toilsome march at an early hour, finding our stock suffering greatly for the want of water. This day we traveled with as much speed as possible, with the hope of finding water whereat to encamp; but at length night arrived, and the fatigues of the day obliged us to encamp without water, wood, or grass. The day had been excessively warm, except when the wind would blow, and in the afternoon two of our dogs died for want of water. On examination we found that the feet of many of our dumb brutes were completely crippled by the sand.

Our situation at present seemed very critical. A dull, gloomy aspect appeared to darken the countenance of every member of the company. We were now completely surrounded with the most aggravating perplexities—having traveled two long days' journey into the plain and no idea how far yet to its termination, and from the manifestations of many of our most valuable stock, we were well convinced they could not endure these hardships much longer. To add vexation to our present difficulties, a violent altercation took place between the men as to whether we would proceed in our present direction, or turn back to the mountain. A majority of the men were in favor of the latter, but Captain Walker, who never done anything by halves, with a few others, were of the opinion that we were half way across, and could as

easily proceed as return. On all such disputes, on all former occasions, the majority decided on what steps should be taken;
but when our Captain was in the minority, and being beloved
by the whole company, and being a man also who was seldom
mistaken in anything he undertook, the men were very reluctant
in going contrary to his will. The dispute created much confusion
in our ranks; but fortunately, about midnight the Captain yielded to the wishes of his men, and as it was cool, and more pleasant
traveling than in the day time, we started back towards the
mountain, intending to follow the same trail, in order to come to
the hole at which we encamped on the first night in the plain.[83]

Previous to starting, we took the hides off our dead cattle
and made a kind of moccasin for such of our beasts as were lame,
which we found to be of great advantage, as it effectually
shielded their feet from the scouring effects of the sand.[84]

Nothing happened through the night, and we moved carelessly
along our trail, as we thought; but our feelings cannot be described at daylight when no signs of our former tracks could be
discovered. Men were despatched in every direction on search,
but all returned without any tidings with which to comfort our
desponding company. The compass told which direction we
should go, but otherwise we were completely bewildered. Our
horses, cattle, and dogs were almost exhausted this morning.
The pitiful lamentations of our dogs were sufficient to melt the
hardest heart. The dumb brutes suffered more for water than
food, and these dogs, when death threatened to seize them,
would approach the men, look them right in the face with the
countenances of a distracted person, and if no help could be afforded, would commence a piteous and lamentable howl, drop
down and expire. When the day became warm we slackened our
pace, and moved slowly forward, but without any hope of meeting with any water at least for a day longer. When night came

[83] The attempted short-cut across the desert to the Humboldt River thus
failed through lack of drinking water, and the party was forced to turn back.

[84] Buffalo hide "moccasins" were commonly made by the Plains Indians to
protect their horses' feet when they were sore. Undoubtedly Walker remembered
this Indian practice.

we halted for a short time in order to collect the men and animals together, which were scattered in every direction for a mile in width, lest we should get separated at night, as we intended to travel on without ceasing until we would find water or arrive at the mountain.

When our forces collected together, we presented a really forlorn spectacle. At no time, either while crossing the Rocky or California mountains, did our situation appear so desperate. We had to keep our dumb brutes constantly moving about on their feet, for if they would once lay down it would be impossible to get them up again, and we would then be compelled to leave them. Nor were the men in a much better condition. It is true, we had food, but our thirst far exceeded any description. At last it became so intense that whenever one of our cattle or horses would die the men would immediately catch the blood and greedily swallow it down.

When our men had collected together and rested their wearied limbs a little, our journey was resumed, finding that the cattle and horses traveled much better at night than in daylight. We advanced rapidly this evening without any interruption, until about midnight, when our horses became unmanageable, and contrary to our utmost exertions would go in a more northern direction than we desired. After several ineffectual attemps to check them, we thought perhaps it would be well enough to follow wherever they would lead. We had not followed our horses far until we discovered, to our indescribable joy, that the instinct of our horses was far more extensive and more valuable than all the foresight of the men, as we, unawares, came suddenly upon a beautiful stream of fresh water.

We now had the greatest trouble to keep our beasts from killing themselves drinking water—in which we succeeded only in part, and were thus occupied until daylight, when we counted our force for the purpose of ascertaining how much loss we sustained by undertaking to cross the desert, and found that we had lost sixty-four horses, ten cows, and fifteen dogs.

In order to get something to eat for our stock, and also to

keep them from drinking too much water, we left this stream which had afforded such delight, before either the men or beasts had time to repose their wearied limbs. After traveling a few miles this morning we had the good luck to come across tolerable pasture and plenty of wood and water. Here we determined on staying until the next morning, for the purpose of resting our wearied stock.

This desert which had presented such an insurmountable barrier to our route, is bounded on the east by the Rocky Mountains, on the west by the California Mountain.[85] on the north by the Columbia River, and on the south by the Red, or Colorado, River. These two mighty rivers rise in the Rocky Mountains adjacent to each other, and as the former flows in a northwest and the latter in a southern direction, forms this plain in the shape of the letter A. There are numerous small rivers rising in either mountain, winding their way far towards the center of the plain, where they are emptied into lakes or reservoirs, and the water sinks in the sand. Further to the north where the sand is not so deep and loose, the streams rising in the *spurs* of the Rocky and those descending from the California mountains, flow on until their waters at length mingle together in the same lakes.

The California Mountain extends from the Columbia to the Colorado River, running parallel with the coast about one hundred and fifty miles distant, and twelve or fifteen hundred miles in length with its peaks perpetually covered with eternal snows. There is a large number of water courses descending from this mountain on either side—those on the east side stretching out into the plain, and those on the west flow generally in a straight course until they empty into the Pacific; but in no place is there a water course through the mountain.

The next morning after finding the pasture, our herd having rested and satisfied their hunger pretty well, we resumed our journey along the edge of the plain, traveled as fast as their weakened state would admit of, still finding pasture sufficient for

[85] Leonard's "California Mountain" is, of course, the Sierra Nevada Range.

their subsistence, until, after several days' constant traveling, we fortunately came to our long sought for passage to the west. This was hailed with greater manifestations of joy by the company, than any circumstance that had occurred for some time, as it gave us to know where we were, and also to know when we might expect to arrive in a plentiful country of game. Here we again layed by a day for the purpose of resting, and making preparations to follow our old trail towards the Great Salt Lake.[86]

June 8th. This morning we left the California Mountain, and took a northeast direction, keeping our former path, many traces of which were quite visible in places. Here vegetation is growing rapidly, giving our herd abundant pasture, in consequence of which they have greatly improved in appearance, and are enabled to travel quite fast. After continuing our course in this direction for a few days without interruption, we at length arrived in the neighborhood of the lakes at the mouth of Barren River, and which we had named Battle Lakes. All along our route from the mountain this far, we had seen a great number of Indians, but now that we had reached the vicinity of the place where we had the skirmish with the savages when going to the coast, they appeared to us in double the numbers that they did at that time; and as we were then compelled to fight them, by their movements now, we saw that this would be the only course for us to pursue. We had used every endeavor that we could think of, to reconcile and make them friendly, but all to no purpose. We had given them one present after another—made them all the strongest manifestations of a desire for peace on our part, by promising to do battle against their enemies if required, and we found that our own safety and comfort demanded that they should be severely chastised for provoking us to such a measure. Now that we were a good deal aggravated, some of our men said hard things about what they would do if we would again come in contact with these provoking Indians; and our Captain

[86] The Walker party was now on familiar ground and could retrace their steps of the previous year to the Humboldt Lake region (Leonard's "Battle Lakes") and up the Humboldt River (his "Barren River") with confidence.

was afraid that, if once engaged, the passion of his men would become so wild that he could not call them off, whilst there was an Indian found to be slaughtered. Being thus compelled to fight, as we thought, in a good cause and in self-defense, we drew up in battle array, and fell on the Indians in the wildest and most ferocious manner we could, which struck dismay throughout the whole crowd, killing fourteen, besides wounding a great many more as we rode right over them. Our men were soon called off, only three of whom were slightly wounded.[87]

This decisive stroke appeared to give the Indians every satisfaction they required, as we were afterwards permitted to pass through the country without molestation. We then continued our course up Barren River, without meeting with anything to interrupt us, until about the 20th of June, when we found that if we continued in this direction our provisions would become scarce long before we would reach the Rocky Mountains; and accordingly on the 21st our Captain decided on leaving this river and taking a northern direction for the purpose of striking the headwaters of the Columbia River, where we would find game plenty, and also beaver.

After leaving Barren River we made a quick passage across the country and the first waters we came to was Lewis River, near its head, where we found game such as deer, elk, bear, and beaver plenty.[88] After laying in a small stock of fresh meat here, we resumed our journey towards the buffalo country. On the morning of the 3d of July we were delighted by seeing some buffalo in company with four of our Spanish cattle that had strayed a short distance from the main body during the night, two of which our hunters killed, being the first we had seen since we left the Great Salt Lake the year before. We traveled a short dis-

[87] This battle appears to have been almost a repetition of the conflict with the Paiutes in the same general Humboldt Lake area on the expedition's westbound journey. Again Walker became convinced that the large number of Indians following his men constituted a threat to their safety, and he ordered an attack upon those Indians to disperse them so that his party might pass safely through their country.

[88] The passage was from the upper waters of Humboldt River to those of the Snake (Leonard's "Lewis") River.

tance today when on arriving at a large spring of most delicious water situated in a beautiful grove, where we concluded to spend the National Anniversary of American Independence; and accordingly our hunters went out in the afternoon and killed several very fat buffalo, which were dressed and the choice parts prepared for a grand feast on the morrow. When the morn of the glorious *fourth* first dawned we gave three salutes, spent the morning in various kinds of amusement, and at noon partook of our national dinner, which was relished the better as we had a small portion of good old brandy, which we drank in a few minutes, deeply regretting that we had not a small portion of what was that day destroyed by the millions of freemen in the States. The remainder of the day was celebrated by drinking toasts, singing songs, shooting at mark, running, jumping, and practicing on our horses—having the two Spaniards still with us, who learned us many singular pranks, and were a valuable addition to our company, as they created a great deal of fun and were always in a good humor.

July 5th. Today continued in search of Captain Bonneville,* on Bear River, in finding whom we succeeded without having much difficulty, on the 12th, after traveling through a luxuriant, though rather rough country—where we again had intercourse with people of our own nation, being the first we had met with, except the crew of the *Lagoda*, since we separated from these same men at the Great Salt Lake.[89] Here we encamped for the purpose of resting a few days, and probably remaining until we would receive supplies of provisions, merchandise, &c., from St.

* This name has heretofore been printed *Bowville*—by mistake.

[89] Captain Bonneville's account of his meeting with Walker's party on Bear River suggests that this reunion may have taken place at a slightly earlier date:

"Pursuing his course up Bear River, Captain Bonneville arrived, on the 13th of June, at the Little Snake Lake; where he encamped for four or five days. . . . Having finished his survey of the lake, Captain Bonneville proceeded on his journey, until on the banks of the Bear River, some distance higher up, he came upon the party which he had detached a year before, to circumambulate the Great Salt Lake, and ascertain its extent, and the nature of its shores. They had been encamped here about twenty days; and were greatly rejoiced at meeting once more with their comrades, from whom they had been so long separated." (Irving, *Adventures of Captain Bonneville*, 384.)

Lewis—spending our time in discussing the many scenes encountered by each of us, and the many hair-breadth 'scapes that
such-and-such a one had made.

After remaining in this situation a few days, there arrived at
our camp a company of twenty-five men belonging to the British
North-West Fur Company, from Fort Vancouvre, situated near
the mouth of the Columbia River.[90] These people informed me
that the infant colony at the mouth of the Columbia River had
revived, and was now increasing rapidly, under the superintend-
ence of the British, and contained one hundred and fifty families,
the major part of which are English, Canadian, French and Indians, and but few Americans. They carry on agriculture to a
considerable extent—the soil being very fertile, climate mild, and
frost and snow but seldom known. They also have a grist and
saw mill, and are establishing an extensive fishery at the mouth
of the river, for the purpose of catching salmon, as they are very
abundant in this stream. They have a governor, and live under
a republican form of government. From all accounts, however,
their government is not of much use, as the most unbounded
freedom of action is exercised by all the members of the colony,
and their government is intended more for effect with the Indians than any advantages to the people.

About the 17th of July this party left us and continued their
journey in search of the Blackfeet Indians for the purpose of
trading—after which they said it was their intention to return
to the coast by the same route.

We remained here until the 20th without meeting with anything particularly, when Captain Cerrie joined us with forty
men, bringing a large supply of merchandise packed upon mules
and horses from Missouri. With what we had on hand these men
brought enough merchandise and provision to supply our present company for a whole year. This party intended to return
immediately to Missouri with what peltries we had on hand.

These succoring companies are always looked for with great

90 The men were employees of the Hudson's Bay Company, which had absorbed the North West Company in 1821.

anxiety by the people who have been in the mountains any length of time. Many are at times entirely destitute of such articles as would be of great advantage to their comfort—many expect letters or some other manifestations of remembrance from their friends—besides some, who have been strictly temperate (because they could not help it, as the supply of liquor will always be exhausted) look forward with longing anticipations for the supply which is always sent to this country by the owners of these companies, for the purpose of selling it to the men and thus paying their wages. It is generally brought in a refined state, and is a cash article, which they retail at the enormous price of one dollar per gill. Generally when a succoring company of this kind arrives at the camp of the trapper, the men get a little mellow and have a real jubilee—with the exception of a few (after the Indian fashion) who are always prevented, as they must watch the rest and keep a look-out lest the whole company should be surprised and massacred by the Indians. Scarcely one man in ten of those employed in this country ever think of saving a single dollar of their earnings, but spend it as fast as they can see an object to spend it for. They care not what may come to pass tomorrow—but think only of enjoying the present moment.[91]

We now began to make the necessary arrangements for our future operations—such as dividing such men as wished to remain in the mountains into one company, and such as wished to return to the States in another, and settling with the men for the last year's services, and hiring them for the ensuing year.

July 30th. Having every necessary arrangement completed,

[91] Irving (*Adventures of Captain Bonneville*, 407), described the actions of the mountain men following Mr. Cerré's arrival at the rendezvous: "The arrival of the supplies gave the regular finish to the annual revel. A grand outbreak of wild debauch ensued among the mountaineers; drinking, dancing, swaggering, gambling, quarreling, and fighting. . . . A camp, recovering from one of these riotous revels, presents a serio-comic spectacle; black eyes, broken heads, lack-lustre visages. Many of the trappers have squandered in one drunken frolic the hard earned wages of a year; some have run in debt, and must toil on to pay for past pleasure. All are sated with this deep draught of pleasure, and eager to commence another trapping campaign."

Mr. Cerrie returned to the state of Missouri with forty-five men, and what fur, &c., we had in store. Captain Bonneville was left to make his fall hunt on the headwaters of the Columbia River and the adjacent country with fifty men, and Captain Walker with fifty-five men, being the balance of our force, to cross the Rocky Mountains to the waters of the Missouri River, and then continue hunting and trading with the Indians until the month of June, 1835,[92] when Captain Bonneville with his men would join us on the Bighorn River, at the mouth of Popoasia Creek,[93] which empties into the Bighorn below Wind River Mountain.

After the usual ceremony of parting on such occasions, which is performed by each one affectionately shaking hands all round —we separated, each division taking off in a separate direction. Captain Walker continued up Bear River in an eastern direction, and the first night encamped at Smith's Fork. In the morning we resumed our journey in the same direction, being the most direct route to the summit of the mountains, nothing occurring more than usual with the exception of killing any quantity of game we might think proper, until about the 8th of August, when, as the company were passing through a small prairie, we discovered a large grizzly bear laying in the shade of some brush at the edge of the woods, when four of us started for the purpose of killing him, but on coming close, the bear heard us and ran into the thicket. We now took separate courses, intending to surround the bear and chase him out and have some sport; but one man, as we came to the thicket, acted very imprudently by dismounting and following a buffalo path into the brush, when the bear, hearing our horses on the opposite side, started out on the same path and met the man, when he attempted to avoid it by climbing a small tree, but being too closely pressed was unable to get out of the reach of the bear, and as it passed, caught him by

[92] Bonneville claimed that Walker returned to St. Louis with Cerré and the furs collected during the year, and that the party to the Crow country was led by Montero (The Huntsman). (Irving, *Adventures of Captain Bonneville,* 408.) However, Leonard makes it quite clear that the party dispatched to the Crow country was under Walker's leadership.

[93] This is the Popo Agie ("Head River"), so named by the Crow Indians.

the leg and tore the tendon of his thigh in a most shocking manner. Before we could get to his aid the bear made off and finally escaped.

Here we encamped and remained until the next day, when the wounded man expired—having bled to death from the wound, although every effort in our power was of no use. After burying this man, which was done in the customary manner of interring the dead in the mountains—having dug a deep hole in the ground, into which we deposited the body well wrapt up in blankets, and then filled up the grave, first with bark and then with earth, we continued our journey a short distance in the afternoon and encamped on the headwaters of Lewis River, and at the base of the Rocky Mountains.

Here we made preparations for our voyage across the mountains. Few that have once performed a journey across these hills will encounter them a second time with a cheerful spirit; and particularly will they dread the task if they have encountered as many hardships and perils as some of the company that now reposed at its base, silently contemplating the dreadful fatigues to be encountered until we would reach the eastern base.

In the morning at an early hour we left the waters which empty into the Pacific, and continued our way up the mountain, which we found tolerable rough, and covered, in places, with a large quantity of snow. We traveled without ceasing, and without meeting with any interruption, until we at last arrived in the Prairies, on the east side, near the headwaters of the Yellowstone River.[94] On our passage across, we found several pieces of petrified wood, one of which was six or eight feet long—which our men divided amongst themselves, for the purpose of making whetstones. Here we concluded on commencing our fall's hunt, as the beaver appeared to be quite numerous.

In the neighborhood of the headwaters of this river, the country is generally composed of prairie hills, covered with excellent

[94] Merrill J. Mattes has suggested that the Walker party crossed the Rockies via the Pacific Creek–Two Ocean Pass–Atlantic Creek route. ("Jackson Hole, Crossroads of the Western Fur Trade 1830–1840," *The Pacific Northwest Quarterly*, Vol. XXXIX, No. 1, [1948], 19.)

grass, and abound with plenty of game of different kinds. After trapping here a few days, we agreed to move down onto Wind River, which empties into Yellowstone a short distance below this,[95] and whilst leisurely traveling along one day through an extensive prairie, a large horde of buffalo were discovered at a distance making towards us with considerable speed. No one was disposed to take any notice of them, as we had plenty of provision, until we seen them advance closer and faster, as if they were going to ride right over us. The whole drove came rushing past, at which our loose and pack horses took fright, and started in advance of the buffalo, scattering our baggage in every direction over the prairie for several miles, leaving us nothing but our riding horses. This occasioned us to encamp for the purpose of collecting our stray horses and lost baggage, which was done, with the exception of one horse and some merchandise, which we were unable to find. To see a drove of perhaps a thousand buffalo driving through a level plain as fast as their strength will permit them, is a most frightful spectacle; and then, when our horses started in advance, pitching and snorting, the scene was beyond description. Many of our horses were severely crippled in consequence of this chase—so much so that we were detained three days in waiting on them and repairing our injured merchandise.

A few days after leaving this place we arrived, Aug. 20, on Popoasia Creek, where we found an oil spring rising out of the earth similar to that of any other spring. After emptying into the creek, the oil can be seen floating on the surface for a considerable distance. The oil is of a dark hue when in the fountain, almost like tar, but is as thin as water. If this spring was in the States, I have no doubt the chemist might make a valuable use of it. A Mr. Bergen, belonging to our company, and who had been severely afflicted with the rheumatism, procured a phial of it, which he used, and afterwards said it afforded him entire relief.

[95] Wind River empties into the Bighorn and the Bighorn into the Yellowstone. Leonard here refers to the mouth of the Wind River, not the Bighorn.

Aug. 21st. Today we continued in pursuit of beaver, which is our daily occupation, passing from one water course to another, through plains and over hills, all of which are prairie, with the exception of the base of the mountain, where there is an abundance of timber. We traveled in this manner, and spending our time mostly in this way, without meeting with any misfortunes, or anything unusual in a backwood's life, occasionally being quite successful in catching beaver, until near the middle of October, when we arrived among the tribe of Crow Indians.[96]

We now find the weather getting cold, with plenty of snow, frost, and ice, which compels us to suspend our trapping for this season, having done a very fair business; and to increase our store of peltries, we now commenced trading with these Indians for buffalo robes, beaver fur, &c., for which purpose we intend passing the winter in this neighborhood.

After remaining here a few days, in the meantime obtaining the principal part of the valuable peltries of the Indians, the company left them and appointed Wind River as the place to meet and resume the trading as soon as the Indians could collect a supply—leaving two men and myself among the Crows for the purpose of instigating them in the business of catching beaver and buffalo.

Nov. 1st. This morning Captain Walker and his followers left us and continued in the direction of Wind River, there to erect a temporary trading house for the winter season, and we remained with the Indians who were engaged in collecting their winter's supply of meat, which is the custom of all tribes in a plentiful country of game, to go in bodies sufficiently large to defend themselves in case of an attack by a neighboring hostile tribe, as there is scarcely three tribes to be found in the whole Indian country on friendly terms with each other.

[96] The Crow Indians, a Siouan tribe, were renowned among the tribes of the Upper Missouri for their fine dress and their wealth in horses. They were bitter enemies of both the Blackfeet and the Sioux. Although they stole horses from the trappers, they could brag that they had not murdered any white men. The Crows and their culture were first described by the Canadian trader François Larocque, who traveled with them in the summer of 1805, in his *Journal of Larocque from the Assiniboine to the Yellowstone, 1805.*

I now found myself in a situation that had charms which I had many times longed for. Ever since I engaged in the trapping business, I had occasional intercourse with the Indians, but never resided with them until now; which would afford me every opportunity to minutely observe their internal mode of living. The Crows are a powerful nation, and inhabit a rich and extensive district of country. They raise no vegetation, but entirely depend on the chase for a living. This is the situation of nearly every tribe, and when game gets scarce in one part of the country claimed by a certain tribe, they remove to another part, until after a while their game becomes scarce, when they are induced to encroach upon the territory of a neighboring tribe, which will at once create a fearful strife, and not unfrequently ends in the total destruction of some powerful nation.[97]

It will be recollected that I was amongst these Indians once before, when some of our horses were stolen and we followed them into the Crow village, where we found our horses and also a Negro man, in the winter of 1832–33. This man we found to be of as great advantage to us now as on former occasions, as he has become thoroughly acquainted with their language, method of transacting their public and private business, and considered of great value by the Indians. He enjoys perfect peace and satisfaction, and has everything that he desires at his own command.[98]

The Crow Nation contains from seven to eight thousand souls, and are divided into two divisions of an equal number in each—there being too great a number to travel together, as they could not get game in many places to supply such a force.[99] Each division is headed by a separate chief, whose duty it is to pilot

[97] The Crows, situated between the aggressive Blackfoot tribes on the north and the powerful Sioux on the east, were in greater danger of total destruction than any other tribe of the Upper Missouri at that time.

[98] This was the mulatto, Edward Rose. See footnote 31.

[99] Contemporaries of Leonard estimated the Crow population at about four hundred lodges. The two divisions of the Crows were the River Crows, who generally resided in the Yellowstone Valley, and the Mountain Crows, who preferred the high country farther south. Long Hair was head chief of the Mountain Crows. (Edwin T. Denig, *Of the Crow Nation,* 24, note 6.)

them from one hunting ground to another, and to lead his followers to battle in time of war—one of whom they call Grizzly Bear and the other, Long Haired Chief, which name he derives from the extreme length of his hair, which is no less than nine feet eleven inches long. This is the principal chief, or Sachem, of the nation, and is quite a worthy and venerable looking old man of seventy-five or eighty years of age. He uses every possible precaution to preserve his hair, which is perfectly white, and has never had it cut since his infancy. He worships it as the director or guide of his fate through life—never rising or laying down without humbly and devoutly adoring this talisman, and which they term *Bah-park* (medicine).[100]

It is customary for every tribe of Indians in the regions of the Rocky Mountains to have some instrument or article to pay homage to and invoke, but no nation, I believe, are so devoutly attached to their talismans as the Crow Nation—it is their life— their very existence. Almost every individual of the Crow Tribe has something of this kind, and which generally consists of a seed, a stone, a piece of wood, a bear or eagle's claw, or anything which their fancy may lead them to believe has a successful virtue, and which has been purchased of some noted warrior who has been successful in his undertakings whilst in the possession of such an article. This magical thing, whatever it may be, is carefully enveloped in a piece of skin, and then tied round their neck or body. If an old experienced warrior gives one or two young men an article of this kind on going to war, and they happen to be successful in taking scalps or stealing horses, the whole affair is attributed to the virtue of his talisman, and he can then sell it for almost any price he demands, and if it be a precious stone, or seed, or piece of wood, all similar articles are immediately enhanced in value, and the greater the price they pay for such an article, the greater service it will be to them in the

---

[100] "The Long Hair" was the first signer of the first treaty between the Crow Indians and the United States, negotiated at the Mandan Villages, August 4, 1825. The length of his hair has been variously given as from 9' 11" to 36'. He died a few years prior to 1856. (Denig, *Of the Crow Nation*, 63, and footnote 40.)

From a lithograph in Forbes, *History of Upper and Lower California,* 1839

Lassoing Cattle in California

By Captain William Smyth, 1822

Crow Indian Warrior

A Painting by George Catlin, 1832

hour of need. Some of them will even give four or five good horses for the most trifling and simple article of this kind.

Their principal wealth consists of horses, porcupine quills, and fine dressed skins, for clothing, &c., but nothing is of so much value as their idols; without which an Indian is a poor, miserable drone to society, unworthy the esteem and companionship of brutes. Long Haired Chief worships nothing but his hair, which is regularly combed and carefully folded up every morning into a roll about three feet long by the principal warriors of his tribe.

Their houses are composed of dressed buffalo hides and pine poles about twenty-five or thirty feet in length, and about three inches in diameter. These poles are stuck upon end in a circle, and all coming together at the top form the shape of a hay-stack. The buffalo robes are then cut in proper shape, sewed together, and covered over their habitation. Their fire is placed in the center of the lodge, and the poles being left apart at the top afford a very good draught for the smoke. Some of these houses are much larger than others, such as are intended for the transacting of public business. These are constructed with much care, and are quite comfortable and convenient habitations—the buffalo robes affording a sufficient shield from the effects of the cold. In their public buildings all their national affairs are discussed at stated periods by the warriors and principal men. Here they have their public smokes and public rejoicings.

This tribe is also governed by a species of police, such as having a committee of soldiers appointed for the purpose of keeping order and regulation in their village, appointing a day for a general hunt, and keeping any who might be so disposed from running ahead and chasing off the game, in order that each individual may have a fair chance to obtain an equal share of provision, with his neighbor. These soldiers are also to observe that on such occasions their village is not left in a weak and unsafe condition by too many going to war, or to horse stealing (which generally ends in war) at a time, and also to see that such a party is properly provided with a competent commander, and if not, it is their duty to supply the deficiency by appointing one to act in his place. If any person acts contrary to their laws, these soldiers have the liberty of punishing him for it, which is done by shaving his horse's mane and tail, cut up his lodge, and whip him, if not contrary to the decision of the principal chief, in whom is invested the power of vetoing every act of this executive committee if not agreeable to his wish.

When game becomes scarce, and they are about to move to another section, every movable article is packed upon horseback, when they travel on until they arrive in a country abounding with game. Their children from two to three years of age, and unable to ride, are tied upon the baggage, and those younger are fastened upon a board and conveyed in manner as heretofore described. They have a sort of dray formed by these poles, which is done by fastening one end to the pack saddle, and the other end dragging on the ground, on which they place their furniture.

There is more personal ambition and rivalry existing among this tribe than any other I became acquainted with—each one trying to excel the other in merit, whilst engaged in some dangerous adventure. Their predatory wars afford them every opportunity for this, as they are at liberty and sometimes compelled to engage in the battle's strife as soon as they are able to bend the bow or wield the tomahawk. Their first promotion from the ranks of a private citizen is secured by stealing a few horses and killing one or two of their enemies, when they are eligible to the title of a Small Brave. By adding so many more acts of this kind, they receive the title of a Large or Great Brave; from thence to a Little Chief, and to rise to the station of a Great Chief, they must steal such a number of horses, kill and scalp such a number of the enemy, and take so many guns or bows and arrows.

Whenever one person exceeds the existing chief in these deeds, he is installed into the office of chief of the nation, which he retains until some other ambitious, daring brave exceeds him. They always take good care, however, not to excel their present chief, old Long Hair.

This school, as it was, creates a great deal of jealousy and envy among the people, but it seldom leads to any disturbance, as the executive soldiers, or police, are always ready to chastise and punish any such conduct.

Any person not rising to either of these stations by the time he is twenty years of age, has nothing to say or do in any public business whatever, but is compelled to perform different kinds of menial labor altogether degrading to a man, as it is putting him on an equality with the squaws—which is low enough indeed in the estimation of the Indian. Such a man becomes the slave of the women, as they are at liberty to order him to do anything they may think proper, such as carry wood, water, &c., or any drudgery that is required to be done.

After receiving the title of Little Chief they are at liberty to speak and take part in all public debates in relation to the affairs of the nation, and are exempt from all kinds of labor in going to war, which has to be done by the privates, who are generally young men, as on such occasions they have no women with them; and as they progressively rise, they are at liberty to order and command those who are beneath them. This is the principal cause of their ambition, which far exceeds description. If one of the men who has fallen into the rank of a woman, and has become tired of that occupation, he will undergo any exertion, and encounter any danger, no matter how great, in order to distinguish himself and improve upon his forlorn and dishonorable condition.[101]

Soon after we took up our quarters with these Indians, I occupied my time in ascertaining their manner of taking game, which, if it is more laborious, it is more successful than the Spanish mode of taking wild horses. When their families are in want of provision, or desirous of having a hunt, one of the principal men, who might be called the *Trumpeter*, will mount a horse and ride round through the encampment, village, or settlement, and publicly proclaim that on a stated day the whole tribe must

[101] The late Robert H. Lowie, a leading authority on the Crow Indians, had a high regard for most of Leonard's information about this tribe. However, he regarded Leonard's statements about tribal government as "interesting, though not wholly convincing." (Lowie, *The Crow Indians,* 336.)

be prepared for a general hunt, or *surround*. When the day arrives, the village is alive betimes in the morning, and several hundred will sometimes mount their race horses and repair to a certain designated section of country, which they are to surround. When the men have all had time to get to their allotted stations, they begin to close in, driving the game, principally buffalo, into a circle and when they are pretty well confined in the circle, they commence killing them—until which time, no man dare attempt to take any of the game. In this manner they have sometimes caught several hundred buffalo, besides many other animals, at a single surround.

When they are in a country suitable, these people will destroy the buffalo by driving a herd of some hundreds to the edge of a convenient rocky precipice, when they are forced headlong down the craggy descent. This is more dangerous than the other method, as the buffalo, unless the Indians are very numerous, will sometimes rush in a solid column through their ranks, knocking down the horses and trampling their riders under their feet.

They have another method of taking buffalo, which is in this way:—If they know of a place at the base of some mountain that is surrounded on three sides with inaccessible precipices, and a level valley leading into it, they manage to drive the whole gang of buffalo into this neck and force them up to its termination, when they erect a strong fence across the valley, or outlet, and then butcher their prisoners at leisure.

In a place of this kind I was shewn by the chief Grizzly Bear, upwards of seven hundred buffalo skulls which he said had been caught at a single hunt, and which had taken place about four years previous.

About the 20th of November, after traveling for three or four days in pursuit of provision, we at length arrived in the vicinity of buffalo, where we pitched out tents and the Indians prepared for a general hunt. In the evening their horses were all dressed in the best style, and at an early hour the next morning four or five hundred Indians were mounted and ready for the chase.

This was a favorable opportunity for me to gratify my curiosity in seeing this kind of sport, and my companions and myself followed in the rear of the Indians. Our hunters had not advanced far on this sporting expedition until they met with an object which entirely put them out of the notion of showing us their agility in catching buffalo, for, at some distance across the plain, along the base of some rough craggy hills, was espied a considerable body of people, who appeared to be advancing towards us. Immediately a halt was called, for the purpose of observing the movements of the strangers, and consulting on what steps should be taken. It did not require the keen eye of a Crow Indian long to tell that their visitors were Indians and belonged to their implacable enemies, the Blackfeet Tribe. This was enough. War was now their only desire, and our Indians advanced towards their enemies as fast as the speed of their horses would admit, who, being on foot, were soon overtaken and forced to ascend the rocks, which they did in safety. The Crows immediately surrounded the Blackfeet, confident of an easy victory, but when they made the attack they found that their enemy was too well prepared for defense, and they immediately despatched an express to the village for a reinforcement of men, conscious that the Blackfeet would not attempt to leave their present position until such reinforcements would have time to arrive.

This was quite a different kind of sport from that which I expected to witness when I left the Indian camp, but one of no less interest, and far more important to me. Whilst the express was absent both parties employed their time in strengthening their positions—the Blackfeet had chosen a most fortunate spot to defend themselves, and by a little labor found themselves in a fort that might have done credit to an army of frontier regulars. It was situated on the brow of a hill, in a circle of rocks shaped similar to a horseshoe, with a ledge of rocks from three to four feet high on either side, and about ten feet, on the part reaching to the brink of the hill, with a very creditable piece of breast-work built in front, composed of logs, brush, and stones. From

145

their present situation they have a decided advantage over the Crows, and if well prepared for war, could hold out a considerable length of time, and deal destruction thick and fast on any force that might attempt to scale their fort—which looks more like the production of art than nature. Whilst the Blackfeet were assiduously engaged in defending their position, the Crows were no less idle in preparing for the attack, the destruction of which, they were determined should not be relaxed as long as there was a living Blackfoot Indian to be found in the neighborhood. Previous to the arrival of the reinforcement, which was about ten o'clock, there had been three Crows and one Blackfoot killed, which was done at the first attack after the latter were driven into their fort.

When the express reached the Crow village, every man, woman and child able to point a gun or mount a horse repaired with all speed to the scene of action, who came up uttering the most wild and piercing yells I ever heard in my life. A great deal of contention at first took place among the principal men of the Crow Tribe as to the manner of attacking their enemy, who appeared to look down upon them in defiance; notwithstanding the Crows kept up a continual yelling and firing of guns, all of which was without effect. Finally they appeared to harmonize and understand each other.

As matters now seemed to indicate the approach of a crisis, I repaired to an eminence about two hundred yards from the fort among some cedar trees, where I had an excellent view of all their movements. At first the Crows would approach the fort by two or three hundred in a breast, but on arriving near enough to do any execution, the fire from the fort would compel them to retreat. They then formed in a trail along the top of the ridge, and in rotation would ride at full speed past the breastwork, firing as they passed, and then throwing themselves on the side of the horse until nothing will be exposed to the enemy except one arm and one leg. This they found to be very destructive to their horses and also their men, there being now ten Crows and several horses laying dead on the field. Urged by their ill success thus far, and by the piteous lamentations of the wives, children, and relatives of those who had fell, the Crow chiefs decided on suspending the attack, and determined to hold a council of war for the purpose of deciding on what measures should be adopted, in order to destroy these brave Blackfeet.

When the principal chiefs met in council, all was still except the lamentations of the bereaved, who, perhaps, regret the severe pennance which the customs of their people compelled them to endure for the memory of a deceased friend, and lament more on account of the prospect of trouble ahead than for the loss which they have sustained. The chiefs held a hasty and stormy council. Some were in favor of abandoning the Blackfeet entirely, and others were determined on charging into their fort and end the battle in a total and bloody massacre. This was finally decided upon, but not until after several speeches were made for and against it, and the pipe of war smoked by each brave and chief.

As soon as this determination of the chiefs was made known, the war whoop again resounded with the most deafening roar through the plain—every voice that was able to make a noise was strained to its very utmost to increase the sound, until the very earth, trees, and rocks seemed to be possessed of vocal powers. By their tremendous howling they had worked as great a change in the courage of their soldiery as the most soul-enlivening martial music would the cowardly fears of a half-intoxicated militia company.

Now was the moment for action. Each man appeared willing to sacrifice his life if it would bring down an enemy; and in this spirit did they renew and repeat the attack on the breastwork of their enemy, but as often did they retreat with severe loss. Again and again did they return to the charge, but all was of no use—all their efforts were of no avail—confusion began to spread through their ranks—many appeared overwhelmed with despair —and the whole Crow nation was about to retreat from the field, when the Negro, who has been heretofore mentioned, and who had been in company with us, advanced a few steps towards

147

the Crows and ascended a rock from which he addressed the Crow warriors in the most earnest and impressive manner. He told them that they had been here making a great noise, as if they could kill the enemy by it—that they had talked long and loud about going into the fort, and that the white men would say the Indian had a crooked tongue, when talking about his war exploits. He told them that their hearts were small, and that they were cowardly—that they acted more like squaws than men, and were not fit to defend their hunting ground. He told them that the white men were ashamed of them and would refuse to trade with such a nation of cowards—that the Blackfeet would go home and tell their people that three thousand Crows could not take a handful of them—that they would be laughed at, scorned, and treated with contempt by all nations wherever known—that no tribe would degrade themselves hereafter by waging war with them, and that the whole Crow Nation, once so powerful, would forever after be treated as a nation of squaws. The old Negro continued in this strain until they became greatly animated, and told them that if the red man was afraid to go among his enemy, he would show them that a black man was not, and he leaped from the rock on which he had been standing, and looking neither to the right nor to the left, made for the fort as fast as he could run. The Indians guessing his purpose, and inspired by his words and fearless example, followed close to his heels, and were in the fort dealing destruction to the right and left nearly as soon as the old man.

Here now was a scene of no common occurrence. A space of ground about the size of an acre, completely crowded with hostile Indians fighting for life, with guns, bows and arrows, knives, and clubs, yelling and screaming until the hair seemed to lift the caps from our heads. As soon as most of the Crows got into the fort, the Blackfeet began to make their escape out of the opposite side, over the rocks about ten feet high. Here they found themselves no better off, as they were immediately surrounded and hemmed in on all sides by overwhelming numbers. A large number on both sides had fallen in the engagement in the inside of the fort, as there the Crows had an equal chance with their enemy, but when on the outside the advantage was decidedly against them, as they were confined in a circle and cut down in a few moments. When the Blackfeet found there was no chance of escape, and knowing that there was no prospect of mercy at the hands of their perplexed and aggravated, but victorious enemy, they fought with more than human desperation. From the time they left their fort, they kept themselves in regular order, moving forward in a solid breast, cutting their way through with their knives, until their last man fell, pierced, perhaps, with an hundred wounds. In this massacre, if one of the Blackfeet would receive a dangerous wound he would drop to the ground, as if dead, and if his strength was not too far exhausted, he would suddenly rise to his feet and plunge his knife to the heart of an enemy who would be rushing through the crowd, and then die. This would not be done in self-defense, nor with a hope of escape, but through revenge.

This was truly a scene of carnage, enough to sicken the stoutest heart—but nothing at all in comparison with what took place afterwards. The Crows, when they found the enemy strewed over the field, none having escaped their vengeance, commenced a general rejoicing, after which they retired a short distance for the purpose of taking repose and some refreshment.[102]

Although the victory was complete, the Crows paid dear for it, having lost about thirty killed and as many more wounded, besides a great number of horses. The loss of their companions did not appear to dampen the rejoicing of the men the least bit, and indeed it would appear that the squaws should do all the mourning and lamenting, as well as all the labor. Their dead were all collected together, when the squaws went round and claimed their kindred. This was a most affecting scene—but what was it

[102] Another mulatto, James Beckwourth, also lived among the Crow Indians. In his account of his experiences he appears as the hero in a great number of battles with the Blackfeet, including the one described by Leonard above. (T. D. Bonner, *The Life and Adventures of James P. Beckwourth, Mountaineer, Scout, and Pioneer, and Chief of the Crow Nation of Indians,* Chapter XVI.) However, Beckwourth was a young man in his middle twenties in 1834. He could not have been the "old Negro" referred to by Leonard.

when contrasted with that enacted by the men as soon as they had rested from the toil of battle. The women would throw themselves upon the dead bodies of their husbands, brothers, &c., and there manifest the most excruciating anguish that any human being could suffer. The women were occupied in this manner when the men went to work to glut their merciless vengeance on their fallen foe.

Many of the Blackfeet who were scattered over the battle ground had fallen by broken limbs or wounded in some way, and were yet writhing in agony, unable to injure anyone or help themselves in any way. All such were collected together, and then tormented in a manner too shocking to relate. These fiends would cut off their ears, nose, hands, and feet, pluck out their eyes, pull out their hair, cut them open and take out part of their insides, piercing them with sharp sticks—in short, every method of inflicting pain was resorted to. In order that they might render their mode of torment still more excruciating, they would bring into the presence of the dying the bodies of those who were already dead, and then tear out their hearts, livers, and brains, and throw them in the faces of the living, cutting them to pieces, and afterwards feeding them to their dogs—accompanying the whole with the most taunting and revengeful epithets, whilst those not engaged in this fiendish work were occupied in keeping up a constant screaming, howling, and yelling. When this torment commenced, all the sufferers who could get hold of a knife or anything with which they could take away their lives, would do so immediately. All the torment that could be inflicted by their persecutors failed to bring a single murmur of complaint from the sufferers—nor would they signify the least symptoms of being conquered. No—not if they had been offered undisturbed liberty, would those sufferers who had lost so many of their companions, acknowledge themselves prisoners in the Crow village. Death they preferred to this, and death with indescribable horrors did they all receive.

After they had finished tormenting the living, which was not done until there was no more to kill, they commenced cutting off the heads of the mangled bodies, which were hoisted on the ends of poles and carried about, and afterwards dashed them against trees, rocks, &c., leaving them on the plain to be devoured by wild beasts.[103]

The men now repaired to their dead friends, where they went through various manoeuvres, as much as to say that they had revenged their death, and soon afterwards everything was on the move towards the camp, where we arrived soon after dark, not to rest, and calmly meditate on the scenes of the day, but to see further developments of the superstitious propensities of the poor neglected savage.

Arriving in the village, a part of the men commenced their public rejoicings by beating upon drums, dancing and singing, which, together with the incessant wailings and lamentations of those who had lost relatives, gave us a night that was entirely free from repose and averse to sober reflection. In this manner the whole night was spent, nor did the morning bring any prospect of a cessation of these singular customs.

About ten o'clock the whole tribe was engaged in performing the funeral obsequies to the remains of their deceased relatives. At an early hour the wife had seated herself by the side of her dead husband, where she would remain until it came his turn to be interred, when she would clasp the cold and lifeless form of him, whom she still seems to love, and cling to it until forced away by some of the men. Their manner of burying their dead is also most singular in some respects: The corpse is carefully wrapped up in buffalo robes and laid into the grave, together with his talisman, and anything else to which he was attached, and if he be a chief of some importance, his horse's tail and mane are shaved off and buried with him—these benighted Indians believing that each of these hairs will turn into a beautiful horse in the land of spirits, where they think that a horse and

---

[103] Both the torture of prisoners and the mutilation of the bodies of dead enemies were practiced also by the Blackfeet in their wars with the Crows and other tribes. These "indescribable horrors" commonly followed a bitter battle in which a number of warriors of the victorious party were killed.

bow and arrow are all that a man requires to perfect his happiness and peace.

As soon as the dead were deposited in the silent tomb, the musicians collected together and marched through the camp, beating upon sticks and drums as a signal for the mourners to fall in the rear, which they did, and the whole procession then proceeded to the top of some rising ground, not far off, where the males and females separated into different groups. The female mourners now took the point of an arrow, which was fixed in a stick, and commenced pricking their heads, beginning at one ear and continuing round the forehead to the other, making incisions half an inch apart all round; and the men went through a similar course on their legs, arms, &c., until the blood oozed out in streams. All this performance was done without creating the least appearance of pain.

After doing this each female that had lost a near relative or particular friend collected along a log and deliberately cut off a finger at the first joint, which was done with as much coolness as the pricking process. This is done by the males also, except the two first fingers on the right hand, which they preserve for the purpose of bending the bow, and many of the aged females may be seen with the end off each of their fingers, and some have even taken off the second crop.[104] Whilst this was being done by the mourners, the other Indians kept up a continual noise with their music, singing, dancing, and yelling.

The procession now returned to the village with the faces of the female mourners daubed over with their own blood, which they never remove until it wears off. Those not wishing to lose

---

[104] Edwin T. Denig, who knew the Crows for nearly two decades prior to 1856, described their sacrifices of fingers in mourning for dead relatives: "This is done by placing an ax or butcher knife on the joint, and striking the same with a good-sized stick. Occasionally, in a high state of excitement, they lay their finger on a block and chop it off with a knife held in the other hand. The blow often misses the joint and the finger is divided between joints, which takes a long time to heal and leaves a portion of the bone protruding which presents a very disagreeable appearance. . . . They never tie up these sores, but after daubing over their faces with the blood, hold a bunch of wild sage on the stump until it stops bleeding." (*Of the Crow Nation*, 35.)

a finger are at liberty to shave off their hair close, but it is the general custom among the Crows to lose a piece of their finger. Anyone who has lost a relative is not allowed to take part in the dance or any kind of sport for twelve or thirteen moons, unless one of their surviving friends take the life of an Indian belonging to the tribe that killed the mourned one—which will at once atone for all loss and drown all grief, and she is then allowed to wash the blood from her face and resume her former standing in society. This night was spent in about the same manner as last night—some being engaged in dancing and singing, and others crying and lamenting the loss they had sustained.

Nov. 22d. This morning the chief of the nation gave orders to move for the purpose of getting among the buffalo and other game—and also to be prepared for a national dance on their march. About ten o'clock the whole tribe was in readiness and we started in the direction of the battle ground, and on arriving there a halt was ordered for the purpose of giving the dead carcasses of the Blackfeet the last evidence of the Crows' revenge—which was done by beating and mangling every piece of flesh they could find. This done, the march was resumed to a beautiful level plain, perfectly smooth and covered with short grass, for two or three miles square—where the national dance was to take place. When they had dismounted, the whole nation formed a ring, when sixty-nine of the oldest squaws, all painted black, formed themselves in a line in the center of the circle, each bearing a pole from twelve to fifteen feet in length. The person who struck the first blow at their late battle with the Blackfeet now commenced dancing and was immediately followed by every young man and woman belonging to the tribe (except the mourners, who stood silent, melancholy spectators) all clad in their best dresses, handsomely worked with porcupine quills, and their heads delightfully ornamented with magpie and pheasant tails—forming themselves in double file and dancing round the whole circle to wild, though not irregular, music—which they make by stretching a piece of buffalo skin over a hoop similar to a riddle, where it is well stretched, and then sewed together and

153

filled with sand and left until it is dry and properly shaped, when the sand is thrown out and some pebbles or bullets put in, when it is ready for the hand of the musician—and is in shape similar to a gourd.

After dancing round the circle once or twice, they would suddenly halt, shout their terrible war-whoop—shoot off their guns, when the rattling music would again commence and they would all be engaged in the dance. Each member of the tribe who was not mourning, from the child up to the enfeebled old man and woman took part in this exercise.[105] After about two hours spent in this manner, they concluded their celebration by the display of an Indian battle, which was exceedingly grand, far beyond any description I had ever heard. Seventy or eighty of their best warriors mounted their most active horses, one party acting the part of their enemies, the Blackfeet, each one armed with a gun, a club or lance, and some with both. They separated, one party to one side and the other to the other side of the plain, and at a given signal would advance towards each other as fast as their horses would run, firing and striking as they would pass—throwing themselves nearly under their horses, so much so that they could fire at each other under their horse's belly. During the time they seemed to exert every nerve, yet they kept up a continual noise, by repeating the most wild and ferocious yells I ever heard. Their activity in throwing the lancet is no less wonderful—being so expert in this business that they can throw it twenty to twenty-five yards and strike a mark the size of a man's head, whilst riding past as swift as their horses will go.[106]

The greater part of the day was occupied in this manner, after which they took up their march towards the river No-Wood, on the banks of which stream we encamped for the night. In this vicinity buffalo appeared to be quite numerous and the Indians killed several this evening. As the prospect of game ap-

[105] This was the Crow version of the scalp dance. The women's blackened faces indicated that enemies had been killed.

[106] The Crow Indians were reputed to have been the best horsemen of all the Upper Missouri tribes.

peared so good, the Indians determined on remaining here a few days for the purpose of laying in a stock of buffalo robes to trade with Captain Walker. The Indians would go out in large companies and kill a great number of these animals, when it would be the duty of the women to follow after and gather up the hides, which they would convey to the camp and dress them ready for market. It is the duty of the squaws to dress the buffalo robes alone, which is done by stretching the hide tight on the ground and there let it dry, when they have a piece of iron or sharp stone, fixed in a stick, making a tool similar to a foot-adze, with which they cut and scrape the fleshy side until it becomes thin and smooth—after this they have a mixture composed of the brains and liver of the animal mixed together, in which they soak the hide a couple of days, when it is taken out and again stretched on the ground, where it is beat and rubbed with a paddle until it becomes perfectly soft and dry.

After catching a good many buffalo and some beaver at this place, we removed towards the point designated to meet Captain Walker and his men. On the 30th we encamped at the junction of the Bighorn and Wind rivers. Not long after dark our encampment was surprised by a party of about fifty Blackfeet suddenly appearing among our horses for the purpose of stealing them. This created a great uproar in our camp. Every Indian was on his feet and ready for fight in an instant. The enemy was discovered too soon, and had to retreat with the loss of one man, without taking any horses at all. They were followed a great ways across the plain to the mountain, but as the night was very dark they could not be overtaken, and finally escaped. The one who had fallen was a principal chief among the Blackfeet, and had ventured too near the encampment for the purpose of choosing a valuable horse.

Here we were to have another scene of Indian exultation. On the former occasion, when the sixty-nine Blackfeet had been killed, there was too much grief mingled with the joy of the Crows to render it anything like complete; but now it was quite different—an enemy had fallen without costing a drop of blood on their part. On the former occasion it was joy only imitated—now it was exultation in reality. It appears natural for these Indians to exult more over the death and scalping of one enemy without the loss of one of their own than they would to kill fifty of the enemy and lose one of their own.

After those who had given chase to the Blackfeet returned to camp, this dead Indian was taken in hands. After everyone had carefully examined him, he was taken to a tree and there suspended by the neck, when the men commenced shooting at him and the squaws piercing him with sharp sticks. This work was kept up until after midnight, when they commenced dancing and singing, yelling and shouting, which was carried far beyond that of the 21st and 22d November. In this manner they spent their time until near ten o'clock, when they prepared to remove up Wind River—which they did after all taking leave of the dead Indian by abusing it in some manner to show their spite.

We traveled up Wind River until the 4th of December when we arrived at the camp of Captain Walker, whom, together with his men, we found in good health and spirits. This camp is situated sixty or seventy miles east of the main chain of the Rocky Mountains, on the headwaters of Wind River, which, after running one hundred and fifty or two hundred miles in an eastern direction, empties into the Bighorn. The Wind River Valley, through which this river passes, is one of the most beautiful formations of nature. It is upwards of twenty miles wide in some places, and is as level as a floor, with the margin of the river evenly ornamented with thriving cottonwood. A great many white people pass the winters in this valley, on account of the abundance of buffalo and other game.

The first night after reaching the camp of my old companions was spent in telling and hearing told the many exploits and adventures which we had severally seen and took part in since our separation. Captain Walker and his men had passed the time without encountering any hardships, or being disturbed in any way, with the exception of a party of hostile Indians who watched

Crow Indian Woman in Mourning

A Painting by George Catlin, 1832

The Adventurous Captain Bonneville

their movements for some time and who at last succeeded in stealing a few of their horses.

The following day the Crow chiefs were made presents of some small articles of merchandise, when we commenced bartering with them for their furs and buffalo robes. As soon as they had sold out their present stock, they left us, all highly pleased with their success, and commenced hunting for more. As game was very plenty here, we determined on spending the winter in this valley, where we occupied our time in hunting and trapping a little ourselves, but deriving our principal profits by trading with the Indians for robes, which they would bring into our camp as fast as they could dress them.[107]

The daily hunting of the Indians, as well as ourselves, had thinned the buffalo pretty well, and driven them across the country onto the Platte River—in consequence of which the Indians are now (1st March, 1835) preparing to leave us and go down to the Yellowstone River, which empties into the Missouri, where they intend spending the summer.

The Indians left with us one of their tribe who had received a stroke of palsy, or a similar affliction, which had deprived him of speech and of the use of one-half of his body. He was a man of thirty or thirty-five years of age, appeared to be in good health, but was entirely helpless, one arm and one leg, being entirely numb, or dead, and beginning to decay. He was entirely speechless, and had been in this situation for four years. They told us that this man had been a great warrior, and that the morning after returning from a hard, though successful battle, he was found in his bed dead, as they supposed, and that, when about to bury him in the evening, he gave signs of remaining life— when he was conveyed back to his wigwam, and remained there for two days and nights, when he recovered to the situation in which he was left with us. As he had been such a valuable chief, they did all in their power to restore him the use of his body, and had conveyed him about with them from place to

[107] The Mountain Crows commonly wintered in sheltered locations in the Wind River Valley.

place ever since, but had resolved to do so no longer, and therefore left him with us, telling us to do with him as we pleased—if we saw proper to take him with us well and good, if not, we might leave him to be food for the beasts of the forest.

Having concluded our winter's hunt and trading with these Indians, who have left us, our men are now occupied in digging holes for the secretion of our peltries and merchandise, until we return from our spring's hunt, and when we would be joined by Captain Bonneville and his company, who was to meet us at the mouth of Popoasia Creek in June next. On the 8th I was sent by the Captain to measure the size of the holes that the men were digging and whilst in one of them, taking the dimensions, with three other men, the bank caved in, covering two men entirely, another up to the shoulders, and dislocating my foot. Of the four, I was the only one that was able to get out without assistance—the others being all seated at the time the accident happened. Help was immediately obtained, and the men extricated as soon as possible, who appeared entirely lifeless, but after rubbing and bleeding them effectually, they recovered, when the men proceeded to extricate the one whom we thought was the least injured, but whom we found to be in the most dangerous situation, as his legs and lower part of his body was completely crushed. This man (Mr. Laront, of St. Louis, where he left a wife and four children) suffered most severely during the remainder of the day and all night, and died the next morning about sunrise.

The manner of digging these holes is upon a high, dry bank, where they sink a round hole like a well, five or six feet, and then dig a chamber underground, where the merchandise is deposited—after which the *well* part of it is filled up, and the top covered with the natural sod, and all the overpluss earth is carefully scraped up and thrown into the river, or creek, so that nothing may be left on the premises to lead to the discovery of the hidden treasure.

March 10th. Today we deposited in the cold earth the remains of our lamented companion, Mr. Laront, in the most respectable manner our means would allow, after which we resumed our business of secreting our stores. Our provisions were again growing scarce, for which purpose each one is anxious to be on the move. When we first came to this place, we could stand in our encampment almost any morning and shoot down some lazy buffalo that would be lurking in the neighborhood—but now our hunters might scour the valley a whole day and not kill as much as a rabbit.

Having everything in readiness for removing on the morning of the 12th, Captain Walker went to the palsied Indian and told him that we were about going and were not able to take him with us. The poor Indian then, not being able to speak, made imploring signs to us to leave him as much provisions as we could spare. This we did with cheerfulness, but it only consisted of the carcass of a wolf, which we placed within reach of him, when he requested that we would fasten the cabin door so as to prevent the entrance of wild beasts.

The wounded, consisting of one with a broken leg, another's back sprained, and myself my foot dislocated, were placed on a litter made of a buffalo skin, with a pole tied to each side of it and fastened between two horses. This was the most painful traveling to me, as well as to the others, that I had ever experienced—particularly whilst passing over a rough piece of ground.

Our course led in a northern direction after reaching the Bighorn River, which we followed a few days and then crossed over to Tongue River, which stream empties into the Missouri below the mouth of the Yellowstone. Here we decided on hunting and trapping, as beaver signs were quite numerous. The ice had not entirely melted from this stream yet, but there was none left to prevent us from following our favorable pursuit. In this neighborhood, we spent the months of April, May, and part of June, passing from one watercourse to another, finding plenty of beaver at each place, and some other game. During the whole time we were permitted to follow our business without any disturbance. All the wounded had completely recovered, and were enabled to make a profitable hunt—having visited, in our toilsome occupation, the headwaters of the following rivers all of which are the tributaries of the Missouri—Tongue, Powder, Yellowstone, Little and Big Porcupine, Musselshell, Priors, Smith's, Gallatin's, Otter, Rosebud, Clark's, and Stinking rivers.[108]

About the 10th of June we suspended our trapping and returned to Wind River, where we found Captain Bonneville and his men waiting for us according to appointment, at the mouth of Popoasia Creek.[109]

Here we encamped for a few days, until we could collect our peltries together and make a divide—having sent some of our men to bring our merchandise, &c., from the place where we had deposited it, who succeeded without any difficulty, and stated that no traces of the palsied Indian we had left there could be discovered. We now set about packing and sorting our furs, &c., and making arrangements for the ensuing year—such as paying off hands, hiring them for another term, and apportioning the different companies. Captain Walker, with fifty-nine men, was to continue trapping in this country for one year from this time, and Captain Bonneville, with the remainder, taking all the peltries we had collected, and which were packed upon horses and mules, was to go to the States and return in the summer of 1836, with as strong a force as he could collect, and a large supply of merchandise, and meet Captain Walker in this neighborhood.[110]

On parting this time, many of the men were at a loss to know what to do. Many were anxious to return to the States, but feared to do so, lest the offended law might hold them responsible for misdemeanors committed previous to their embarking in the

[108] Although most of these streams are tributaries of the Yellowstone, the Musselshell is a tributary of the Missouri, and the Stinking (Water), the present Shoshone River, a branch of the Bighorn.

[109] The united parties of Captain Bonneville "celebrated the 4th of July, in rough hunters' style, with hearty conviviality" at the rendezvous on the Popo Agie. (Irving, *Adventures of Captain Bonneville*, 493.) Irving also gives a brief résumé of the adventures of Bonneville's party in the Crow country the previous fall, winter and spring (*Adventures of Captain Bonneville*, 487–492.)

[110] Although Walker remained in the mountains for several years, Bonneville never returned. He sought reinstatement in the army, and on April 22, 1836, President Jackson restored him to the rank of captain.

trapping business, and others could not be persuaded to do so for any price—declaring that a civilized life had no charms for them. Although I intended to return to the mountains again, I was particularly anxious to first visit the States lest I should also forget the blessings of civilized society, and was very thankful when I found myself in Captain Bonneville's company, on the march towards the rising sun. As we traveled along we killed all the game we could, this being necessary, as provision is very scarce on the course we intended to pursue between the village of the Pawnee Indians and the white settlements. About the 25th of July we arrived on the Platte River, which we followed down until we arrived at the Pawnee Village, situated about one hundred and fifty miles from where the Platte River empties into the Missouri. After trading with these Indians for some corn, we left them and traveled rapidly every day until we arrived in Independence (Mo.), which is the extreme western white settlement, on the 29th of August, 1835—after being absent four years, four months, and five days.[111]

FINIS

[111] Irving described the return of Bonneville's party "to the frontier settlements on the 22d of August":

"Here, according to his own account, his cavalcade might have been taken for a procession of tatterdemalion savages; for the men were ragged almost to nakedness, and had contracted a wildness of aspect during three years of wandering in the wilderness. A few hours in a populous town, however, produced a magical metamorphosis. Hats of the most ample brim and longest nap; coats with buttons that shone like mirrors, and pantaloons of the most ample plenitude, took place of the well-worn trapper's equipments; and the happy wearers might be seen strolling about in all directions, scattering their silver like sailors just from a cruise."—*Adventures of Captain Bonneville*, 493.

EDITOR'S BIBLIOGRAPHY

Aldrich, Lewis Cass. *History of Clearfield County, Pennsylvania.* Syracuse, N. Y., 1887.

Bonner, T. D. *The Life and Adventures of James P. Beckwourth, Mountaineer, Scout, and Pioneer, and Chief of the Crow Nation of Indians.* New York, 1856.

Caldwell, J. A. *Caldwell's Illustrated Combination Historical Atlas of Clearfield County, Pennsylvania.* Condit, Ohio, 1878.

Catlin, George. *Letters and Notes on the Manners, Customs, and Condition of the North American Indians.* 2 vols. London, 1841.

Chittenden, Hiram Martin. *The American Fur Trade of the Far West.* 3 vols. New York, 1902.

Conner, Daniel Ellis. *Joseph Reddeford Walker and the Arizona Adventure.* Edited by Donald J. Berthrong and Odessa Davenport. Norman, Oklahoma, 1956.

Cox, Ross. *The Columbia River.* Edited by Edgar I. and Jane R. Stewart. Norman, Oklahoma, 1957.

Dale, H. C. (ed.) *The Ashley-Smith Explorations and the Discovery of a Central Route to the Pacific, 1822–1829.* Cleveland, 1918.

Dana, Richard Henry. *Two Years Before the Mast.* New York, 1840.

Denig, Edwin T. *Of the Arickaras,* Missouri Historical Society Bulletin, Vol. VI, No. 2 (1950). Edited by John C. Ewers.

———. "Of the Crow Nation," Bureau of American Ethnology *Anthropological Paper No. 33, Bulletin 151.* Edited by John C. Ewers. Washington, 1953.

Ewers, John C. *The Blackfeet: Raiders on the Northwestern Plains.* Norman, Oklahoma, 1958.

———. *The Indian Trade of the Upper Missouri Before Lewis and Clark: An Interpretation,* Missouri Historical Society Bulletin, Vol. X, No. 4 (1954).

———. "When the Light Shone in Washington," *Montana, the Magazine of Western History,* Vol. VI, No. 4 (1956).

Ferris, W. A. *Life in the Rocky Mountains.* Edited by Paul C. Phillips. Denver, 1940.

Forbes, Alexander. *California, a History of Upper and Lower California.* San Francisco, 1937.

Glenn, Allen. *History of Cass County, Missouri.* Topeka, 1917.

Gregg, Josiah. *Commerce of the Prairies.* Ed. by Max L. Moorhead. Norman, Oklahoma, 1954.

——. *Diary and Letters of Josiah Gregg.* Edited by Maurice Garland Fulton. 2 vols. Norman, Oklahoma, 1941, 1944.

Hafen, LeRoy R., and Ghent, W. J. *Broken Hand: The Life Story of Thomas Fitzpatrick, Chief of the Mountain Men.* Denver, 1931.

Haines, *The Nez Percés.* Norman, Oklahoma, 1955.

Hodge, Frederic Webb (ed.). *Handbook of American Indians North of Mexico,* Bureau of American Ethnology Bulletin No. 30. 2 vols. Washington, 1912.

Irving, Washington. *The Adventures of Captain Bonneville, U.S.A. in the Rocky Mountains and the Far West.* New York, 1868.

Larocque, François. *Journal of Larocque from the Assiniboine to the Yellowstone, 1805.* Canadian Archives Publication No. 3. Ottawa, 1910.

Leonard, Zenas. *Narrative of the Adventures of Zenas Leonard.* Edited by Milo Milton Quaife. Chicago, 1934.

——. *Adventures of Zenas Leonard, Fur Trader and Trapper, 1831–1836.* Edited by W. F. Wagner. Cleveland, 1904.

Lowie, Robert H. *The Crow Indians.* New York, 1956.

Mattes, Merrill J. "Chimney Rock on the Oregon Trail," *Nebraska History,* Vol. XXXVI, No. 1 (1955).

——. "Jackson Hole, Crossroads of the Western Fur Trade, 1807–1829," *Pacific Northwest Quarterly,* Vol. XXXVII, No. 2 (1946).

——. "Jackson Hole, Crossroads of the Western Fur Trade, 1830–1840," *Pacific Northwest Quarterly,* Vol. XXXIX, No. 1 (1948).

Merriam, C. Hart. "The Buffalo in Northeastern California," *Journal of Mammalogy,* Vol. VII, No. 3 (1926).

Montana Historical Society *Contributions,* Vol. X. Helena, 1941.

Nidever, George. *The Life and Adventures of George Nidever, 1802–1883.* Berkeley, California, 1937.

Ross, Marvin C. *The West of Alfred Jacob Miller.* Norman, Oklahoma, 1951.

Russell, Carl P. *One Hundred Years in Yosemite.* Berkeley, California, 1947.

———. "Wilderness Rendezvous Period of the American Fur Trade," *Oregon Historical Quarterly*, Vol. XLII, No. 1 (1941).

Sublette, William L. Letter in *Missouri Republican*, October 16, 1832. (Regarding Battle of Pierre's Hole.)

Watson, Douglas S. *West Wind: The Life of Joseph Reddeford Walker*, Los Angeles, 1934.

Wollon, Dorothy (Ed.) "Sir Augustus J. Foster and 'The Wild Natives of the Woods,' 1805–1807," *William and Mary Quarterly*, Third Series Vol. IX, No. 2 (1952).

Wyeth, John B. *Oregon: A Short History of a Long Journey.* Vol. XXI in Thwaites' *Early Western Travels, 1784–1897.* 32 vols. Cleveland, 1904–1907.

Wyeth, Nathaniel J. *The Correspondence and Journals of Captain Nathaniel J. Wyeth, 1831–1836.* Edited by F. G. Young. Eugene, Oregon, 1899.

INDEX

Acorns: as food of California Indians, 80, 88, 121

Adams, W. Howard: xxv

American Fur Company: enters the fur trade of the Rockies, xvi

"Arapahee" (Arapaho) Indians: Gantt's trade with, 3, 53

Arikara Indians: trade with, vii, xi; hostility toward traders, xi–xii, 57, 61

Ashley, William H.: in fur trade of the Rockies, x–xiii

Assiniboin Indians: steal trader's horses, x; visit to Washington, 57

"Baggshaw, Capt.": see Bradshaw, Capt. John

Bannock Indians: description of, 48; met by trappers, 65

Bark (cottonwood): as winter horse feed, 13, 25

"Barren River": see Humboldt River

"Battle Lakes," see Humboldt Lake

Battles between trappers and Indians: 21–23, 42–46, 69–72, 75, 130–31

"Bawnack Indians": see Bannock Indians

Bear and bull fighting in California: 110–12

Bear-baiting by Californians: 109–110

Bear River: trappers on, 49–50, 132, 135

Bears: see Grizzly bears

Beaver: trapping of, 11, 20, 27, 48, 58, 63, 68, 136, 137, 159

Bighorn River: 51, 135, 155, 156

Big trees: see Sequoia gigantea

Blackfoot Indians: trade with, viii, 32, 133; warfare with Crows, 145–49, 155–56; warfare with Flatheads, 32; warfare with Shoshonis, 49; warfare with trappers, ix–xi, 32

Blackwell, Capt.: 9, 52; see also Gantt and Blackwell

Bonneville, Capt. B. L. E.: xvi, xviii; career of, 62–63; at 1833 Rendezvous, 62–64; dispatches Walker party westward, 64; at 1834 Rendezvous, 132–33; dispatches Walker party to Crows, 135; at 1835 Rendezvous, 160; returns to Missouri, 160–61

"Bowville, Capt.": see Bonneville, Capt. B. L. E.

Bradshaw, Capt. John: aids Walker party in California, 92–95, 101, 107–108

Bridger, James: xvi

Buffalo: hunting of by trappers, 13, 14, 15, 18–19, 132, 156; range of, 6, 47, 82, 84, 131; stampede of, 137

Burial of a trapper: 46, 158–59

Bush River: see San Joaquín River

Caches, made by trappers: 8, 29, 158

California: Jedediah Smith's overland expeditions to, xiv–xv; Walker party's overland expedition to, 64–132; Indians of, 80, 86–88, 90, 95, 116, 120–22; customs of Mexicans in, 101–107, 109–13; population of, 117

California missions: see San Carlos Borromea and San Juan Bautista

"California Mountain": see Sierra Nevada Mountains

Cattle raising in California: 99–100

Cerré, Michael Sylvestre: assistant to Capt. Bonneville, xvi, 64, 133, 135

Chimney Rock, landmark on Platte River Trail: 7

Colorado River: xii, xiv, 50, 129

Colter, John, first of the mountain men: viii–ix

THE AMERICAN EXPLORATION AND TRAVEL SERIES

of which *Adventures of Zenas Leonard, Fur Trader,* is Number 28, was started in 1939 by the University of Oklahoma Press. It follows rather logically the Press's program of regional exploration. Behind the story of the gradual and inevitable recession of the American frontier lie the accounts of explorers, traders, and travelers, which individually and in the aggregate present one of the most romantic and fascinating chapters in the development of the American domain. The following list is complete as of the date of publication of this volume:

1. Captain Randolph B. Marcy and Captain George B. McClellan. *Adventure on Red River*: Report on the Exploration of the Headwaters of the Red River. Edited by Grant Foreman. Out of print.
2. Grant Foreman. *Marcy and the Gold Seekers*: The Journal of Captain R. B. Marcy, with an account of the Gold Rush over the Southern Route. Out of print.
3. Pierre-Antoine Tabeau. *Tabeau's Narrative of Loisel's Expedition to the Upper Missouri.* Edited by Annie Heloise Abel. Translated from the French by Rose Abel Wright. Out of print.
4. Victor Tixier. *Tixier's Travels on the Osage Prairies.* Edited by John Francis McDermott. Translated from the French by Albert J. Salvan.
5. Teodoro de Croix. *Teodoro de Croix and the Northern Frontier of New Spain, 1776–1783.* Translated from the Spanish and edited by Alfred Barnaby Thomas.
6. A. W. Whipple. *A Pathfinder in the Southwest*: The Itinerary of Lieutenant A. W. Whipple during His Exploration for a Railway Route from Fort Smith to Los Angeles in the Years 1853 & 1854. Edited and annotated by Grant Foreman. Out of print.
7. Josiah Gregg. *Diary & Letters.* Two volumes. Edited by Maurice Garland Fulton. Introductions by Paul Horgan.
8. Washington Irving. *The Western Journals of Washington*

Irving. Edited and annotated by John Francis McDermott. Out of print.

9. Edward Dumbauld. *Thomas Jefferson, American Tourist*: Being an Account of His Journeys in the United States of America, England, France, Italy, the Low Countries, and Germany.

10. Victor Wolfgang von Hagen. *Maya Explorer*: John Lloyd Stephens and the Lost Cities of Central America and Yucatán.

11. E. Merton Coulter. *Travels in the Confederate States*: A Bibliography. Out of print.

12. W. Eugene Hollon. *The Lost Pathfinder*: Zebulon Montgomery Pike.

13. George Frederick Ruxton. *Ruxton of the Rockies.* Collected by Clyde and Mae Reed Porter. Edited by LeRoy R. Hafen.

14. George Frederick Ruxton. *Life in the Far West.* Edited by LeRoy R. Hafen. Foreword by Mae Reed Porter.

15. Edward Harris. *Up the Missouri with Audubon*: The Journal of Edward Harris. Edited by John Francis McDermott.

16. Robert Stuart. *On the Oregon Trail*: Robert Stuart's Journey of Discovery (1812–1831). Edited by Kenneth A. Spaulding.

17. Josiah Gregg. *Commerce of the Prairies.* Edited by Max L. Moorhead.

18. John Treat Irving, Jr., *Indian Sketches*, Taken during an Expedition to the Pawnee Tribes (1833). Edited and annotated by John Francis McDermott.

19. Thomas D. Clark (ed.). *Travels in the Old South, 1527–1860*: A Bibliography. Three volumes. Volumes One & Two issued as a set, 1956; Volume Three, 1959.

20. Alexander Ross. *The Fur Hunters of the Far West.* Edited by Kenneth A. Spaulding.

21. W. Eugene Hollon and Ruth Lapham Butler (eds.). *William Bollaert's Texas.*

22. Daniel Ellis Conner. *Joseph Reddeford Walker and the Arizona Adventure*. Edited by Donald J. Berthrong and Odessa Davenport.
23. Matthew C. Field. *Prairie and Mountain Sketches*. Collected by Clyde and Mae Reed Porter. Edited by Kate L. Gregg and John Francis McDermott.
24. Ross Cox. *The Columbia River*. Edited by Edgar I. and Jane R. Stewart.
25. Noel Loomis. *The Texan–Santa Fé Pioneers*.
26. Charles Preuss. *Exploring with Frémont*. Translated and edited by Erwin G. and Elisabeth K. Gudde.
27. Jacob H. Schiel. *Journey through the Rocky Mountains and the Humboldt Mountains to the Pacific Ocean*. Translated and edited by Thomas N. Bonner.
28. Zenas Leonard. *Adventures of Zenas Leonard, Fur Trader*. Edited by John C. Ewers.